Artists in Profile

CUBISTS

Jeremy Wallis

www.heinemann.co.uk/library
Visit our website to find out more information about **Heinemann Library** books.

To order:

 Phone 44 (0) 1865 888066

 Send a fax to 44 (0) 1865 314091

 Visit the Heinemann Bookshop at www.heinemann.co.uk/library to browse our catalogue and order online.

First published in Great Britain by Heinemann Library, Halley Court, Jordan Hill, Oxford OX2 8EJ, part of Harcourt Education. Heinemann is a registered trademark of Harcourt Education Limited.

Designed by Tinstar Design (www.tinstar.co.uk)
Originated by Ambassador Litho Ltd
Printed by South China Printing Company, Hong Kong, China

ISBN 0 431 11642 3
06 05 04 03 02
10 9 8 7 6 5 4 3 2 1

British Library Cataloguing in Publication Data
Wallis, Jeremy
        Cubists. – (Artists in profile)
        1.Cubism (Art) – Juvenile literature
        I.Title
        709'.0344

Acknowledgements
The Publishers would like to thank the following for permission to reproduce photographs: AKG pp 6, 11, 15, 16, 27, 41, 43, 48, 52; AKG/Walter Limot p 35; AKG/Rabatti-Domingie p 45; L+M Services B.V. Amsterdam 20020801 pp19, 21; Bridgeman Art Library pp 8, 13, 22, 36, 38, 42, 50, 53, 54; Bridgeman Art Library/Lauros-Giraudon p 33; Camera Press/William Vandivert p 40; Corbis Bettman Archive p 18; Corbis/Wood/Graydon p 21; Corbis/Burstein/Barney p28; Corbis/Francis G Mayer p46; Gallerie Martini and Ronchetti/Reunion des Musees Nationaux p 20; Hulton Getty p 10; Museum of Modern Art, New York p 5; Roger-Viollet p 24; Tate Galleries pp 23, 31.

The cover shows *Violin and Guitar* by Pablo Picasso (1913). This image is reproduced with permission of Succession Picasso/DACS ©2002/Corbis.

Our thanks to Richard Stemp for his help in the preparation of this book.

Every effort has been made to contact copyright holders of any material reproduced in this book. Any omissions will be rectified in subsequent printings if notice is given to the Publishers.

Contents

Words appearing in the text in bold, **like this**, are explained in the Glossary.

What is Cubism?

Cubism exploded onto the Paris art scene in the first decade of the 20th century, completely rewriting the rules of painting and sculpture. It is usually credited to three artists: Pablo Picasso, Georges Braque and Juan Gris. So what is 'Cubism'?

For thousands of years artists ignored the 'tricks' their eyes played on them. They ignored recession – where objects far away appear smaller than those close to and where parallel lines seem to join as they extend into the distance. However, from the 14th century artists adopted a fixed viewpoint and rules of **perspective** to create the illusion of three dimensions – height, width and depth – on a flat surface. These rules dominated European art for almost 500 years.

By the end of the 19th century many artists felt hindered by these rules. At the same time the development of photography meant anyone could reproduce a subject. Artists had to do more than simply 'copy' the world. The pioneers of Cubism also believed traditional artistic techniques were failing. They realized that when we experience the world around us we 'see' it in many different ways; some, such as our visual sense, our senses of hearing and touch, are obvious. Others are less apparent: smell and taste, past knowledge and experience. The Cubists wanted to suggest or evoke them in the viewer. They also wanted to make the viewer put his or her own meaning into the art rather than simply look at it.

The French painter Paul Cézanne was an important influence. Cézanne was virtually ignored by the mainstream art world centred on Paris, and painted for most of his life in Provence, in southern France. He believed nature could be reduced to permanent forms: 'Nature should be treated as cylinders, spheres and cones.' In his later works Cézanne made subjects flat and more obviously two-dimensional. He began to ignore perspective and 'tilt' subjects towards the viewer, while maintaining a different viewpoint elsewhere in the picture. These ideas became central to Cubism. In 1907, a year after his death, a Cézanne exhibition was held in Paris. For some, including Georges Braque, it was a revelation.

Braque's L'Estaque paintings captured, according to the art historian JM Nash, 'the essential qualities of Cubism'. Simplified shapes were piled into arrangements of triangles, squares and oblongs. Braque reduced the colours he used to two groups: yellow/brown and grey/green. He later wrote: 'perspective is nothing but an eye-fooling illusion ... which makes it impossible for an artist to convey the full experience of space.' As the Cubists abandoned perspective, it became difficult to judge scale, size and the relationship between objects.

Pablo Picasso brought to early Cubism an interest in primitive art he developed in the two years prior to meeting Braque in 1907. So-called 'primitive art' – from Africa, Latin America, Asia and the Pacific, and the societies of prehistoric and medieval Europe – did not abide by rules of perspective.

Picasso wanted to incorporate primitive art into a painting on a traditional subject. His ideas were radical at a time when western societies believed they were the pinnacle of civilization and culture. Primitive art had been known about for centuries, but few western artists based their style on it. In 1905, Picasso started making preparatory sketches for a large painting of a group of Spanish prostitutes – Les Demoiselles d'Avignon. His most radical step was to base the women's faces on primitive masks. Les Demoiselles d'Avignon is not 'Cubist' but was a turning point for Picasso. It was a way for Picasso to rid himself of European artistic rules.

Picasso and Braque began working on their artistic adventure 'roped together like mountaineers', according to Braque. They showed only a few pieces at select galleries. Juan Gris later joined them. The name 'Cubism' originated in a review of Braque's paintings in 1908. A critic called Louis Vauxcelles complained that Braque had reduced everything to 'Cubes'. Another critic, Charles Morice, then used the name 'Cubism'.

█▌ Les Demoiselles d'Avignon, by Pablo Picasso (1907)
Though Picasso denied seeing African masks until after he had painted Les Demoiselles d'Avignon, *the faces were based on African masks he saw in the Trocadéro in 1907 and ancient Iberian (Spanish) sculptures he saw in the Louvre in 1906.*

Braque, Picasso and Gris created two different phases of Cubism: **Analytic Cubism** and **Synthetic Cubism**. In Analytic Cubism the artists wanted to show that an object looks different from different directions. They knew that they could not show that and at the same time show the way the object looked in real life in a single painting. They decided to focus on showing the object from different angles instead of painting the way the object looked from one particular viewpoint. So, a house might be shown as a simple cube and a pyramid, a violin as the curved edge of the body and a few lines for the strings, a tabletop as a flat square. The artists also used subdued colours because bright colours might distract the viewer from the structure of the picture.

The Synthetic Cubism phase started around 1912. Instead of taking subjects apart, Synthetic Cubism brought different, often **abstract** elements together to create objects. The artists used pieces of newspaper, mirrors and wood, as well as brightly coloured paint. The objects were attached to the paintings so that they made viewers think about the way they were used in real life, but also so that they made up part of the object in the painting. They hoped that this would make their art more realistic.

Picasso, Braque and Gris are often called 'Montmartre Cubists' after the district in Paris where they worked or 'Gallery Cubists' because they only exhibited in small private galleries. Because they worked in seclusion, only vague ideas circulated about what they were doing. Other artists began to create their own interpretations.

Houses at L'Estaque, by Georges Braque (1908)
In 1907 and 1908 Georges Braque travelled to L'Estaque, where Cézanne had often painted. Taking Cézanne's ideas as his starting point, Braque began his own artistic experiments, eliminating all detail and reducing the houses, trees, gorges and viaducts he painted to their most basic shapes.

The Salon Cubists

In 1910, Jean Metzinger, Robert Delaunay, Albert Gleizes and Fernand Léger exhibited at the **Salon d'Automne**. Realizing they were following a similar path, they tricked their way onto the hanging committee for the 1911 **Salon des Indépendants**. Pieces were supposed to be hung in alphabetical order by artist's name, but they arranged for all work by artists with Cubist leanings to be hung in Salle 41 (Room 41) and an adjoining room. Both their outrageous style and blatant rigging provoked uproar. They also generated huge publicity. Reviews described them as 'Cubists' and Cubism was recognized as a school of art. Because they exhibited at the large Paris exhibitions – 'Salons' – they earned the title 'Salon Cubists'. Others joined them and to the public the Salon Cubists were the 'True Cubists', rather than Picasso and Braque.

The Salon exhibitions

For years, major exhibitions had been held annually in Paris. The greatest – the Salon de la Société des Artistes Français – attracted thousands of visitors. However, old-fashioned artists and artistic rules dominated it. The jury selecting exhibition pieces disliked **avant-garde** artists – artists creating radical new art. More tolerant exhibitions were established, including the Salon d'Automne, where **Fauvism** was launched in 1905 and the 1907 Cézanne **retrospective** was held. At the Salon des Indépendants, any artist who paid a fee could exhibit.

The 'Section d'Or'

Several Salon Cubists met regularly at the studio Raymond Duchamp-Villon shared with his brothers Marcel Duchamp and Jacques Villon, in the suburb of Puteaux. The Puteaux artists linked Cubism to the huge technological, scientific, mathematical and cultural changes taking place in France. In 1912, they held an exhibition called the **'Section d'Or'** ('Golden Section'). The name of a Greek theory of proportion, it was also a pun loved by the Duchamps: 'section' also means 'fraternity' so Section d'Or can mean 'golden brotherhood'.

Cubism and the century of change

For years, France – especially Paris – had been recognized as the artistic centre of the world. From around 1900 new social and technological developments inspired both artists and the public. New inventions, such as the car, challenged traditional ideas of time and travel. From 1889, Parisians experienced a revolutionary view of their city – from the Eiffel Tower, then the tallest structure in the world. They saw familiar parks and boulevards as flat surfaces. The Cubists shared the anticipation and optimism felt by many towards the new century.

Of beehives and laundry boats

Cubism is linked to two studio complexes where friendships between artists (and writers and poets) helped the spread of ideas. The River Seine divides Paris. The northern side is known as the Right Bank and the southern as the Left Bank. In Montmartre, on the Right Bank, stood a ramshackle former piano factory nicknamed Bateau-Lavoir (Laundry Boat). Picasso lived here. It was where Braque first saw *Les Demoiselles d'Avignon*. Juan Gris moved there in 1908. La Ruche (The Beehive) was in Montparnasse, on the Left Bank. Artists working there included Alexander Archipenko, Fernand Léger, Henri Laurens, Jacques Lipchitz and Robert Delaunay.

In 1912, Gleizes and Metzinger wrote *Du 'Cubisme'* (*Of 'Cubism'*) – a book that, for many, still defines Cubism. They talked of a 'fourth dimension' – time. The fourth dimension justified their rejection of techniques based on three dimensions, such as traditional **perspective**. Artists could compress time and space by showing several viewpoints at once.

Cubism and politics

Although the last years of the 19th century and the first years of the 20th century were called the *Belle Époque* – the 'fine period' – and despite rising affluence, France experienced much political instability. The 19th century had seen revolutions, war and defeat, and royalist and **republican** upheavals. The working classes demanded a share in prosperity, the freedom to vote and organize trade unions. In 1898, the Dreyfus Affair – when a Jewish army officer was accused of giving secrets to Germany – provoked **anti-Semitism**.

▮▮▮ *The Book*, by Juan Gris (1914) *Juan Gris was a major Cubist innovator and friend of Picasso and Braque. His rigorous analytical mind, scientific education and mathematical leanings drew him close to the* **Section d'Or** *group.*

Right-wing nationalists attacked students and intellectuals as enemies of 'Frenchness'. Anti-foreign sentiments were common. Many hated Germany as a consequence of the **Franco-Prussian War** of 1870–71, when France lost territory to Germany. This fuelled the rush to war in 1914.

In the popular press it was not just that Cubism was not 'realistic' and 'reduced everything to cubes'. The most serious accusation was that Cubism was a 'foreign', somehow German, art (not helped by Cubism's popularity among German collectors, dealers and artists). In 1912, for example, the French parliament discussed Cubism and 'sinister purposes' were attributed to foreign artists.

The propagandists of Cubism

The Cubists owed much of their success to friendly critics, poets and art dealers. Probably the most important was the poet and critic Guillaume Apollinaire (1880–1918). He was an outspoken writer who became Cubism's chief publicist. Daniel-Henri Kahnweiler (1884–1976) was a young German-French art dealer. In 1907 he opened his Galerie Kahnweiler in Paris and soon became an enthusiastic promoter of the Cubists: first Braque and Picasso, later Léger and Gris. He was forced into exile in 1914 and did not return to France until 1920.

World War I (1914–18) and the end of Cubism

World War I marked the end of Cubism, though its influence would be felt for years. Many artists were called up for **military service**, others dispersed around the world. Public hostility towards **avant-garde** art grew. For example, it was alleged that Cubism was a German-Jewish conspiracy to corrupt French values.

Art and society after Cubism

Though most artists involved went on to develop new ideas, the impact of Cubism was huge. And not just on art and artists. Right-wing governments hated avant-garde art. They thought of it as the 'depraved' invention of Jews, 'foreigners', homosexuals and 'Bolsheviks' (followers of Russian socialism). In later years, artists were persecuted, particularly in Germany, where **Expressionism** was labelled '**degenerate**'. Many artists responded. Picasso, Lipchitz, Picabia and Léger referred to the threat of Nazism and Fascism in their work. Some joined left-wing parties, believing they had much in common with progressive political movements.

Cubism had all but ended by 1914, but the anger it provoked caused arguments for years to come.

Alexander Archipenko 1887–1964

- Born 30 May 1887, in Kiev, Ukraine, Russian Empire.
- Died 25 February 1964, New York, USA.

Key cubist works

Walking Figure (1912)
Médrano I (Juggler) (1912–13)
Médrano II (Dancer) (1913)
Head: Construction of Crossing Planes (1913)
Woman with Fan (1914)

Alexander Archipenko was born in Kiev into a well-to-do family. His father, Porfiry Antonvich Archipenko, was a mechanical engineer, inventor and professor of engineering at the University of Kiev. His mother was Poroskovia Wassilievna Machova Archipenko. The family had artistic connections: his paternal grandfather had been a painter of **religious icons**.

Archipenko was privately educated until the age of nine. He then attended the Kiev

Archipenko's early interest in the art of the Italian renaissance helped him combine his love of art with a fascination for engineering and mathematics. He realized that the creative genius of Leonardo da Vinci 'covered art ... [and] science as well as engineering, [and] considered mathematics as the foundation of all arts.'

Gymnasium (high school that prepared pupils for university). His interest in art was first stimulated at thirteen, after a cycling accident left him bedridden for a year. His grandfather gave him a book of drawings by the great Italian **Renaissance** artist Michelangelo, which Archipenko studied and copied.

Archipenko studied art at Kiev University between 1902 and 1905, first painting and later sculpture. The Byzantine icons, frescoes and mosaics of Kiev particularly influenced him. The spirit of the **Russian Revolution** of 1905 encouraged Archipenko to attack his university teachers for being too 'old-fashioned and academic' in their approach to art – to his father's embarrassment. The university expelled him. Archipenko was not upset. He organized his first one-man show the following year, aged only eighteen, before moving to Moscow, the Russian capital. Supported by his family, he stayed for two years and exhibited with various groups.

In 1908, Archipenko went to the **École des Beaux-Arts** in Paris, France. However, he left after only two weeks, finding the academic system restrictive and tedious. Instead, he studied in the Louvre Museum, Paris, which he called his 'real school'. He was especially inspired by the Egyptian, Assyrian, Ancient Greek and medieval displays.

Still only 21, Archipenko took a studio in La Ruche in Montparnasse. From 1909 he worked on the **abstract** figures for which he became famous. In that year he produced several revolutionary sculptures. The following year he began exhibiting at the **Salon des Indépendants**. Little of Archipenko's work at this time was obviously 'Cubist'. However, working at La Ruche and exhibiting at the Salon des Indépendants brought Archipenko into contact with the Salon Cubists. Soon he was incorporating their ideas into his work.

In 1912 he joined the **Section d'Or** and exhibited with them for the next two years. In 1912 Archipenko created what has been credited as the first 'construction' in modern art – a three-dimensional **collage** made of wood, glass, metal and wire. *Médrano I (Juggler)* was rejected by the **Salon d'Automne** and was first exhibited in Budapest, Hungary, in 1913. (It was

destroyed in World War I.) Archipenko created a series of these innovative figures but they were ridiculed in the press.

In 1913, Archipenko exhibited several sculptures and drawings at the **Armory Show** in New York. During World War I, Archipenko lived in the South of France and so avoided **military service** in Russia.

During 1919 he toured extensively and in 1921 finally settled in Berlin and married a German sculptress, Angelica Bruno-Schmitz. There was a growing interest in his work in the USA and in 1923 the Archipenkos travelled to the USA. He established L'École d'Art in New York.

Archipenko lived the rest of his life in New York City. He continued to work until his death on 25 February 1964.

Dance II, by Alexander Archipenko (1914)
From 1913, Archipenko began working on 'reliefs' – carved and painted plaster he called 'Scultpo-Peintures', (Sculpto-Paintings) – and he also completed many paintings, drawings and prints.

Georges Braque 1882–1963

- Born 13 May 1882, in Argenteuil-sur-Seine, near Paris, France.
- Died 31 August 1963, Paris, France.

Key cubist works
Houses at L'Estaque (1908)
Harbour in Normandy (1909)
Le Portugais (The Emigrant) (1911)
Fruit Dish and Glass (1912)
Women with a Guitar (1913)
Glass, Carafe and Newspaper (1913)
Violin and Pipe: Le Quotidien (1913–14)

Georges Braque was born on 13 May 1882, in Argenteuil-sur-Seine, a market town near Paris. His father Charles owned a profitable decorating firm. As a child, Braque was surrounded by artistic influences. Both his father and grandfather were amateur artists (his father enjoyed some success at the Parisian Salon), and Braque often accompanied his father on painting expeditions.

Braque attended the local school. His educational attainments were limited and he claimed to have taught himself art by copying illustrations from popular magazines. At school he did develop a keen interest in sport, especially boxing. (Boxers became a popular Cubist **motif**.) He also played the flute and mastered the violin and accordion.

When he was fifteen, Braque took evening classes at the Le Havre **École des Beaux-Arts**. He befriended aspiring artists Raoul Dufy and Orthon Friesz, who later became members of the **Fauvists**. He did not do well at the École des Beaux-Arts and left in 1899, before the final exams. He began an apprenticeship as a housepainter and decorator, first in the family business and later with a family friend in Paris. As a housepainter, Braque learned several artisans' tricks, such as the imitation of wood grain, which he later used in his Cubist paintings.

His family may have had another motive for apprenticing Braque into the decorating trade. All young Frenchmen were obliged to do **military service**. Skilled artisans had this period of service cut from three years to one. As a qualified decorator, Braque would only need to do one year in the army.

After his year of military service, Braque decided to pursue an artistic career. In 1902, supported by his family, he moved to Paris. He renewed his friendship with Dufy and Friesz and attended a private art school, the Académie Humbert, between 1902 and 1904. In 1903 he also enrolled at the École des Beaux-Arts in Paris, where he encountered Francis Picabia – whom he later described as 'the first painter I'd ever met'. In common with generations of aspiring artists, Braque also spent time studying the art collections in the Louvre – in particular the Egyptian and Greek galleries.

In late 1905 Braque visited the Paris **Salon d'Automne**. He was dazzled by the vibrant paintings of the Fauvists, which included work by his friends Dufy and Friesz. Persuaded to join them, Braque accompanied Friesz to Antwerp in 1906 and, that winter, L'Estaque on the Mediterranean coast, where Cézanne had often painted. In 1907 he exhibited six paintings at the Paris **Salon des Indépendants**. Here Braque met the art dealer Daniel-Henri Kahnweiler, who bought Braque's paintings and signed a contract to be his sole dealer.

Through Kahnweiler, Braque met Guillaume Apollinaire, who, in November 1907, introduced Braque to Pablo Picasso. Picasso had only recently completed his painting *Les Demoiselles d'Avignon*. Braque was both shocked and excited: 'It is as if Picasso has drunk petrol and is spitting fire!' Braque abandoned Fauvism. In response to *Les Demoiselles d'Avignon* he completed his painting *Large Nude* (1908). However, it was the Cézanne exhibition of 1907 that had the most lasting impact. Braque began to concentrate on landscapes, simplifying forms and using restrained colours, rather than the wild and vibrant colours of the Fauves. In 1907 and 1908, he returned to L'Estaque. He began to experiment by eliminating detail and reducing objects to their most basic shapes.

Braque and Picasso became firm friends and worked in studios close to each other in the Parisian district of Montmartre. Picasso provided a wild, impulsive energy, Braque the drive towards ordered geometric forms. 'We saw each other every day, we talked. During those years Picasso and I discussed things which nobody else will ever discuss again, which nobody else would know how to discuss, which nobody else would know how to understand.' Cubism emerged from this unique collaboration. Braque remained a modest man: 'Cubism,' he later explained, 'put painting within the reach of my own gifts.'

■ *Braque was tall, handsome and well built, with a strong physical presence. He was a keen athlete and sportsman, and a skilled amateur boxer; he and several of his friends would often spar together in their studios.*

In September 1908, Braque submitted several canvases to the **Salon d'Automne**. All were rejected. It was reported that the artist Henri Matisse, who was both a member of the jury who decided which pictures should be exhibited and the leader of the **Fauvists**, commented that the pictures were made of 'little cubes'. In November, the critic Louis Vauxcelles reviewed Braque's one-man show at the Galerie Kahnweiler in the newspaper *Gil Blas*. Vauxcelles condemned Braque's L'Estaque paintings: 'The artist ... reduces everything, places and figures and houses, to geometrical schemes, to cubes.' The jibe stuck and in April 1909, the term 'Cubism' was first used by the critic Charles Morice.

In 1911, Picasso and his lover, Fernande Olivier, spent the summer in Céret, a former monastery in the Pyrenees. Braque joined them and he and Picasso cajoled each other to new creative levels. Picasso compared their **avant-garde** artistic partnership to the partnership of the Wright brothers – the pioneers of powered flight – and called Braque 'Wilbur'.

Braque and Picasso were now well into **Analytical Cubism**, which reduced shapes to geometrical structures and depicted objects as if seen from multiple viewpoints. That year Braque stencilled letters into his painting *Le Portugais*. It was a decorator's trick, but it exaggerated the two-dimensional nature of the picture. Picasso began to do the same.

In 1912, aged 30, Braque married Marcelle Lapré – a friend of Fernande Olivier's, whom Picasso had introduced to Braque. The newlyweds rented a house in Sorgues, near Avignon. Picasso and his new lover, Marcelle Humbert, lived nearby. That year Braque created the first **collage** by pasting three pieces of wallpaper to the drawing *Fruit Dish and Glass*. From then on, Braque and Picasso, whose first collages date from a few weeks later, used the technique with increasing invention, introducing lettering, snatches of song lyric, shreds of advertising posters, newspaper headlines, sand and string. This marked the beginning of **Synthetic Cubism**. Braque also began to make paper constructions and sculptures.

In August 1914, World War I began. Braque's collaboration with Picasso ended when Braque was called up for **military service** in the French army. In 1915, at Carency, Braque suffered a serious head wound and was left for dead on the battlefield. He was rescued by doctors the next day, and taken to hospital were he was trepanned – part of his skull was removed in an operation to relieve pressure on the brain. Braque remained in a coma for several days, and recovered consciousness on 13 May – his birthday. After several months in hospital, Braque returned to Sorgues to **convalesce**. He was decorated for bravery and given a medical discharge in 1916.

Meanwhile in Switzerland, Daniel-Henri Kahnweiler – who as a German had been forced to flee France for the duration of the war – was writing a book called *The Rise of Cubism*, which identified Braque and Picasso as the founders of Cubism. Still recovering from his injuries and still too ill to paint, Braque collected together his observations on art. In 1917, these thoughts were put together by the poet Pierre Reverdy and published.

From 1914 onwards, a distance had grown between Braque and Picasso. Several writers in Picasso's circle derided Braque's contribution to Cubism. This angered Apollinaire who, in 1917, wrote a powerful piece insisting that Braque's equal contribution to Cubism be recognized. (Even today, it is Picasso's name that often attaches itself most strongly to Cubism.) In 1917, Braque was horrified to learn that Picasso was designing sets and costumes for ballets and had married an aristocratic Russian ballet dancer. Braque raged against Picasso's surrender to the high life.

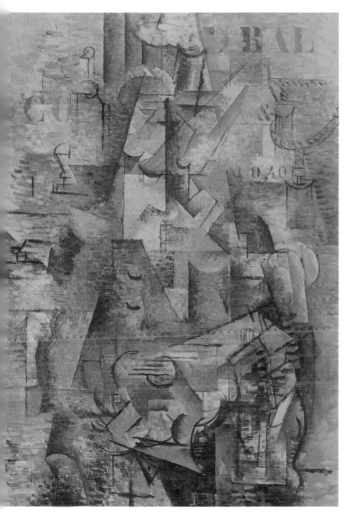

Towards the end of that year, after his long convalescence, Braque began to paint again. Though he completed several geometric pieces, he introduced a gentler, more natural line to his forms. He also began to experiment with engraving, sculpture and lithography.

Le Portugais (The Emigrant), by Georges Braque (1911)
Initially Braque concentrated on landscapes and buildings that automatically gave his paintings a strong, geometrical structure. However, Le Portugais (The Emigrant) *is notable because it is figurative – though it is difficult to see the figure – and is one of the earliest Cubist works to feature stencilled letters and numbers.*

Towards the end of the war there had been a popular campaign for a so-called 'recall (return) to order' in French art and culture to demonstrate its historical roots, strength, continuity and self-discipline. To a great extent Braque embraced these sentiments. By now he was established, his work popular with the wealthy, fashionable elite that shared his modern outlook. Returning to Paris in 1922, he took a studio in the pleasant Montparnasse district.

That year, in line with the 'recall to order', Braque completed a series of paintings of women carrying fruit and flowers based on classical Greek mythology – the *Canéphores (Basket-Carriers)*. He exhibited these, along with sixteen other works, in a room devoted to his art at the 1922 **Salon d'Automne**. Though critical of Picasso for accepting commissions to design sets and costumes for the theatre, Braque also accepted commissions to design for the Ballets Russes in 1923 and 1925.

Glass and Bottle (Fourrures), by Georges Braque (1913–14)
By using collage, Braque created a new relationship between 'true' and 'false'. The materials used were fragments of the 'real world', so were more real than a painted or drawn object – and yet as artworks they were obviously false because the artists were making real fragments play unreal roles in a flat, pictorial world.

Henri Laurens 1885–1954

Henri Laurens was born in Paris, France, on 18 February 1885. He trained as an ornamental sculptor and worked as a stonemason before he decided on a career as an artist. He was mostly self-taught and his earliest artistic works showed the influence of Auguste Rodin. While convalescing from a leg amputation, he met several artists at La Ruche including Fernand Léger and Alexander Archipenko. In 1911 he met Georges Braque, who became his most important artistic acquaintance and a life-long friend. Under Braque's influence, Laurens began to create Cubist **collages** and 'constructions' – collage-sculptures made of various materials such as wire, cardboard, wood, metal, mirrors and so on.

By the 1930s, Laurens had abandoned Cubism in favour of large sculptures cast in bronze. He remained in Paris during World War II where he continued to work. He died on 8 May 1954, in Paris.

During the inter-war years, Braque liked to complete many canvases on a limited number of themes. He also did a series of *Cheminées* – still lifes of objects such as musical instruments and fruit arranged on mantelpieces. In 1928 he reversed this, painting still lifes of pedestal tables laden down with objects usually found on mantelpieces. His first major **retrospective** was in Basel, Switzerland, in 1933. This helped build his international reputation.

In 1940, the Germans invaded France. The Braques fled to the Pyrenees, returning to Paris in the autumn. Prevented from travelling to his country house at Varengeville, Braque withdrew into his studio and produced simple still lifes of domestic objects like washstands and tabletops. After the liberation of France in 1944, Braque returned to Varengeville and resumed his practice of doing series paintings, of billiard tables and studio interiors. In 1945 he was taken ill and had major surgery. During his **convalescence**, Marcelle reported that Picasso was a daily visitor.

Braque was awarded several honours, including the Carnegie Prize and the Venice Biennale Grand Prix for painting. He was made Commander of the Légion d'Honneur in 1958. During the last years of his life, Braque was honoured with important retrospective exhibitions throughout the world, and in December 1961 he became the first living artist to have his works exhibited in the Louvre. He was described, even in old age, as 'the best looking man in Paris'. He remained married to Marcelle Lapré for over 50 years. They had no children. Georges Braque died of old age in Paris, on 31 August 1963.

Robert Delaunay 1885–1941

- Born 12 April 1885, Paris, France
- Died 25 October 1941, Montpellier, France

Key cubist works
Saint-Séverin (1909–10)
The City (1909–11)
The Eiffel Tower (1909–12)
The Windows (1912–14)
Sun, Tower, Aeroplane: Simultaneous (1913)

Robert Delaunay,
by Jean Metzinger (1906)
Though Robert Delaunay claimed that he hated city life, his most famous works were gloriously colourful celebrations of urban life, and he would always have a taste for the good things in life – fine food and wine and comfortable surroundings.

Robert Delaunay was born in 1885 in Paris into a wealthy, cultured family with aristocratic roots. His father, Georges Delaunay, was a successful businessman. His mother, Countess Berthe-Félice de Rose, spent much of her time travelling or socializing with the Parisian elite.

In 1889, when Delaunay was four, his parents divorced. The parting was not amicable and they severed all ties with each other. He spent most of his time with his mother's elder sister and her husband on their country estate near Bourges. He rarely saw his father and only encountered his mother when she returned from her travels. Delaunay loved the countryside and nature, and said he loathed the city and Parisian society.

Delaunay's mother first stimulated his interest in art. Later, at school he proved to be a poor, usually uninterested student, only happy in the art and natural history classes. His attitude caused him to be expelled from schools in both Paris and Bourges. At seventeen, Delaunay told his family he wanted to become an artist. Despite their reservations they agreed to support him.

Delaunay did not immediately enrol at any of the prestigious Parisian art schools. Instead, in 1902, he apprenticed himself to a theatre scenery painter called Ronsin, in a town outside Paris called Belleville. He trained as a decorative theatre set painter with Ronsin for two years. It was Delaunay's only formal training in art, and during this time his mother became his most enthusiastic sponsor. He became a full-time artist in 1904.

Delaunay's early works were inspired by **Impressionism** and **Neo-Impressionism**. He exhibited six canvases at the 1904 **Salon des Indépendants**. In 1908, after completing his **military service**, Delaunay returned to Paris.

In 1909, Delaunay was introduced to Cubism through the gallery of Daniel-Henri Kahnweiler and in the homes of Gertrude Stein and Wilhelm Uhde. During his visits to Uhde's home, Delaunay had been introduced to Uhde's wife, Sonia Terk. She and Delaunay became lovers and married in late 1910. Their son, Charles, was born two months later, in early 1911.

Both the Delaunays believed that, by using different colours, it was possible for an artist to use colour in the same way a composer used musical notes, to create harmonies of colour. Guillaume Apollinaire called Delaunay's colour Cubism **Orphic Cubism**, or 'Orphism'.

Delaunay was a difficult man who worked obsessively on his art, and often neglected himself and his family. They spent most of World War I in Spain and Portugal, where Sonia supported them by working as a theatre and interior designer. Delaunay produced little work of lasting value at this time.

The economic depression of the early 1930s hurt the Delaunays financially. So Delaunay began to paint and exhibit again, which raised his profile and his income. However, in 1938, his health began to fail. He died of cancer in Montpellier, France, in 1941.

▌▌▌ *The Eiffel Tower*, by Robert Delaunay (1910)
Delaunay's deliberate use of the Eiffel Tower was central to his belief in **Simultaneity**. *The Eiffel Tower was actually built as the main radio mast for Paris and France, and as such it was the place where radio communication cancelled all distances out, making it the leading symbol of Simultaneity.*

Sonia Delaunay-Terk 1885–1979

- Born 14 November 1885, Gradizhsk, Ukraine, Russian Empire.
- Died 5 December 1979, Paris, France.

Key cubist works

Blanket (1911)
Bal Bullier (1912–13)
Three Studies for the Electric Prisms (1914)
Marketplace at Minho (1915)

Sonia Delaunay-Terk was born Sofia Ilinitchna Stern on 14 November 1885, into a poor Jewish family in Gradizhsk, Ukraine, where her father worked as a labourer in a nail factory. When she was five, her parents allowed her to be adopted by her mother's brother, Henri Terk. She lived in their home in St Petersburg, shared their cultured way of life and was privately educated.

As a child, Delaunay-Terk was adopted by her wealthy aunt and uncle, Henri and Anna Terk. The family travelled extensively and visited many of Europe's finest museums and art galleries, stimulating her interest in the arts at an early age.

At sixteen, Terk attended a prestigious St Petersburg Gymnasium (high school). Her art teacher recognized her talents and implored the Terks to send her to Germany to study art. They consented, and in 1903, when she was eighteen, she was sent to the Karlsruhe Academy of Fine Arts. In 1905 she moved to Paris, France, where she attended the Académie de la Palette.

Supported by a generous family allowance, Terk threw herself into the exciting Paris art scene. She met an art dealer called Wilhelm Uhde, an important collector and sponsor of **avant-garde** art. On a trip to London in December 1908, to the surprise of their friends, Terk and Uhde married. The union was one of convenience, as it allowed Terk to resist family pressure to return to Russia. Uhde promoted Terk's art in one-woman shows.

In 1909, Terk met Robert Delaunay and they soon became lovers. Uhde and Terk divorced in 1910 and she married Delaunay shortly after. Their son, Charles, was born two months later.

Delaunay-Terk was intimately involved in the development of **Orphism**, but while her husband concentrated on painting, her own work took her in a different direction. She designed **collages**, book covers and furnishings.

Delaunay-Terk was interested in the colour theories of the 19th-century French chemist Michel-Eugène Chevreul who had discovered that our perception of a colour is changed by what colours are next to it. In 1913, she began to produce '**Simultaneous**' clothing made of fabrics with colourful designs. She also opened a shop selling fabrics called Atelier Simultané.

In 1914, while Robert immersed himself in painting, Delaunay-Terk was left to nurse their son through typhoid fever. Until 1917 she had received an income from her family in Russia. However, after the **Russian Revolution**, this income ended. Once Charles had recovered, Delaunay-Terk began to work as an interior designer and theatre designer to support the family.

The Delaunays returned to Paris after World War I. In 1921 Delaunay-Terk collaborated with a **Dadaist** artist called Tristan Tzara on an influential range of women's clothes. She also lectured at the Sorbonne, University of Paris on the influence of avant-garde art on fashion.

After Robert's death in 1941, Delaunay-Terk sold most of her possessions to finance a major **retrospective** of his career. She began to paint again at the start of the 1950s, motivated not least by what she thought was her lack of recognition as an artist in her own right. Due recognition followed – in 1964 she became the first woman to exhibit at the Louvre in her own lifetime. She continued to work until she died peacefully in her studio in Paris, on 5 December 1979.

■ *Contrastes Simultanees,* by Sonia Delaunay-Terk (1912) *As both a painter and a textile designer, Delaunay-Terk spanned the worlds of both avant-garde art and cutting-edge fashion and design. She turned many of her striking artistic ideas into highly successful commercial designs.*

Raymond Duchamp-Villon 1876–1918

- Born 5 November 1876, Blainville, France.
- Died 7 October 1918, Cannes, France.

Key cubist works
Baudelaire (1911)
Maggy (1911)
The Lovers (1913)
The Seated Woman (1914)
Great Horse (1914)

▌▌ *Portrait of Raymond Duchamp–Villon*, by Jacques Villon
A number of Duchamp-Villon's family, including his two brothers Gaston (who adopted the name Jacques Villon) and Marcel, became artists in their own right.

Raymond Duchamp-Villon was born in Blainville, a small town near Rouen, in Normandy, France in 1876. He was the second son of a family of three brothers and four sisters. Duchamp's mother was the daughter of a shipping businessman called Émile Nicole who was also a skilled and well-regarded painter and engraver. The Duchamp family home was filled with examples of his work. Though a full-time mother, Madame Duchamp was an enthusiastic and skilled artist in her own right. She tried to instil this love of art in her children. Duchamp's father was a notary (legal official) who later became mayor of Blainville. He was indulgent and supportive towards his children.

Duchamp grew up in a cultural and artistic environment. He learned musical instruments, was well read, played chess and painted. His decision to become a full-time artist was inspired by his elder brother Gaston.

Like his brother, Duchamp followed an academic route into medicine, all the time attending fine art classes. An accomplished painter, he also fostered a growing interest in sculpture and took it up in 1898. In 1900, after an enforced break from his medical studies caused by a bout of rheumatic fever, he decided he too wanted to concentrate on art full-time and followed Gaston to Paris.

The two brothers' desire to become artists was supported by their parents. Their father agreed to provide them with a regular income by paying out their inheritance in advance. Raymond took the pseudonym Duchamp-Villon after his elder brother's adoption of Villon. Largely self-taught as a sculptor, Duchamp-Villon embraced several more or less conventional styles and exhibited at the **Salon d'Automne** from 1905.

From around 1910 Duchamp-Villon took part in the discussions and arguments that would give rise to the **Section d'Or**. Recognizing the possibilities Cubism presented to the sculptor, he began to eliminate the detail he recorded of his subjects, simplifying them until they were almost **abstract** forms. By 1914 he was recognized as a leading figure amongst the small number of Cubist sculptors.

The final sculptures Duchamp-Villon completed were a series of figures called *Horse*. In 1912, Duchamp-Villon planned a realistic and naturalistic sculpture of a horse and rider. Over the next two years, he reduced his depiction of the horse to that of an abstract representation of its speed and power.

In August 1914, after a one-man exhibition in Paris, Duchamp-Villon was conscripted. Posted near Paris as a medical orderly, he continued working on a plaster version of the fifth and final *Great Horse*.

In 1916, while serving on the front line, he contracted typhus and never fully recovered. He died in Cannes of blood poisoning as a consequence of kidney failure, in October 1918.

Great Horse, by Raymond Duchamp-Villon (1914)
Great Horse was one of a series of sculptures Raymond Duchamp-Villon completed showing the taut, almost machine-like, energy and muscular movement of the horse.

Albert Gleizes 1881–1953

- Born 8 December 1881 in Paris, France.
- Died 23 June 1953 in Avignon, France.

Key cubist works

Landscape (1911)
Woman in a Kitchen (1911)
Harvest Threshing (1912)
The Bathers (1912)
The Football Players (1912–13)
Landscape at Toul (1913)
Portrait of Stravinsky (1914)
Dancer (1917)

Gleizes was born in Paris, in 1881. He was the son of a fashionable and successful fabric designer. He had one sister, Mireille, and was raised in the family home in Courbevoie, a suburb of Paris. He was educated at Collège Chaptal. His career as an artist began after he finished school and was employed in his father's design studio. However, it was during his **military service** between 1901

*Albert Gleizes moved through several artistic styles. In his later work Gleizes tried to adapt the ideas and **motifs** of modern art to express his religious beliefs and devotion.*

and 1905 that Gleizes began to paint seriously. He exhibited for the first time, in Paris, in 1902, at the Société Nationale des Beaux-Arts. In 1903 he exhibited at the **Salon d'Automne**. His early paintings – executed in an **Impressionist** style – showed his concerns for social justice and his deeply held spiritual values.

In 1908 he met Henri le Fauconnier, an artist then experimenting with a very angular style. Though not Cubist, le Fauconnier's style inspired Gleizes to follow a new artistic direction. He adopted a colour scheme and faceting inspired by those of Cézanne, and his style was by now evolving towards Cubism.

Gleizes exhibited at the **Salon des Indépendants** in 1910, along with Metzinger, Delaunay, Léger and le Fauconnier. Though their work was spread out amongst many thousands of exhibits, art critics detected similarities in their work. Recognizing that they shared a similar approach, Gleizes later wrote, 'it seemed essential ... that we should form a group, see more of each other and exchange ideas'. Later that year, at the Salon d'Automne, they exhibited again – putting their work as close to each other's as possible.

That winter Gleizes and the others connived to have their work exhibited together at the 1911 Salon des Indépendants. They took charge of two rooms – Salle 41 (Room 41) and one nearby. Gleizes was the main mover in the plot, and the uproar it provoked led people to refer to the Salle 41 Cubists and speak of a 'Cubist movement'.

In 1912 Gleizes was a founder member of the **Section d'Or**. That same year, he and Jean Metzinger co-wrote the influential book *Du 'Cubisme' (On 'Cubism')*. In 1913 Gleizes's work was included in the influential New York **Armory Show**.

With the outbreak of World War I, Gleizes was again called up to do military service. He continued to paint when he could, and began to execute much more **abstract** works. In 1915 he was wounded in action and in autumn of that year he was discharged from the army. He married a young woman called

Juliette Roche, and they travelled to New York, USA. He exhibited at the Montross Gallery and moved on to Barcelona, Spain, where he held an important one-man show at the Galerie Dalmau in 1916.

In 1917 Gleizes renewed his interest in religion. After returning to France in 1920, he began to write books in which he linked Cubism to 13th-century European religious art. From the mid-1920s, he completed abstract paintings and paintings derived from Cubism on religious themes.

In 1947 **retrospectives** were held in Lyons and Paris. He continued to paint until his death on 23 June 1953, in Avignon, France.

■■■ *Woman at Piano*, by Albert Gleizes (1914)
Gleizes often took as his subjects the modern city, agriculture, work and sport. For example, Harvest Threshing *(1912) and* The Football Players *(1912–13). However, he gradually simplified his style, completing fewer grand landscapes, and painting more intimate scenes, such as* Woman at Piano.

Juan Gris 1887–1927

- Born 23 March 1887, Madrid, Spain.
- Died 11 May 1927, Boulogne-Sur-Seine, northern France.

Key cubist works

Homage to Pablo Picasso (1912)
Violin and Engraving (1913)
The Marble Console (1914)
The Sunblind (1914)
Portrait of Josette Gris (1916)
Harlequin with Guitar (1917)

Juan Gris was christened José Victoriano Carmelo Carlos González-Pérez, and was born in Madrid in 1887, the thirteenth of fourteen children. His father was a Castilian named Gregorio González. His mother was Isabella Pérez, an Andalusian. The family were prosperous – Gregorio González was a merchant – but despite their wealth and social position, most of Juan Gris' brothers and sisters died young. Circumstances later changed and the business was ruined, but Gris was still brought up in a cultured, bourgeois family environment.

At the age of six, according to his sister Antonieta, Gris' interest in art was apparent. From his first day at school he filled the margins of his exercise books with sketches. His school work often suffered as a consequence, and this caused many arguments within the family. Gris did his parents' bidding and buckled down to his studies. Between 1902 and 1904 he studied science, engineering and mechanical drawing at the Madrid Escuela de Artes y Manufacturas (School of Arts and Industries).

He continued to draw, and had several caricatures, cartoons and illustrations published in Madrid newspapers and periodicals. In 1904 he finally persuaded his parents of his commitment to art. They allowed him to abandon his studies to pursue a career as an artist and painter.

In 1906 José adopted the deliberately ordinary pseudonym Juan Gris (the English equivalent would be John Grey). He also decided that Madrid was too restricting. There was nothing new being done there, and many Spanish artists had left the country – mostly for Paris. Moreover, Gris knew he would soon be conscripted into the army. He confided his secret plan to move to France to his sister. They raised what money they could to pay for the journey – even selling Gris' bed and mattress! According to his sister, when he arrived in Paris he had 'just sixteen francs in his pocket', the equivalent today of just a couple of pounds or dollars. He was nineteen years old.

Initially Gris struggled financially, but was too proud to ask his family for help. He showed his illustrations around the offices of several Paris magazines and began to secure commissions. Through his work he got to know several writers and poets, including Guillaume Apollinaire and the poet, Pierre Reverdy. While he was trying to establish himself, Gris was given credit by various shopkeepers, grocers and artists' supply merchants. He would write down his debts in long columns on his studio wall and ask Reverdy to help him add up the columns! Gris also got to know several members of the large expatriate Spanish community. From 1907, he was able to make a living as an illustrator and cartoonist for magazines based in Paris and Barcelona.

In 1908, Gris took a studio in 13 Rue Ravignon – the Montmartre tenement known as the Bateau-Lavoir where Picasso worked. Here he joined the circle of **avant-garde** artists and poets around Picasso that included Braque, Apollinaire and Reverdy. It was here that Gris also met the pioneering art dealer Daniel-Henri Kahnweiler, the exclusive agent for Braque, Picasso and Fernand Léger. According to Kahnweiler, Gris had started painting by this time, but kept his work out of the public eye for four years. (Others say he only started to paint seriously in 1910.) He also took an interest in the work Picasso and Braque were doing.

In 1908, Gris began a short relationship with a young woman who became pregnant. In April 1909 she gave birth to a son, who was christened Georges Gonzáles Gris. Soon after the couple separated, and Georges was sent back to Madrid where he was raised by Gris' sister Antonieta.

Gris' earliest artistic efforts were still lifes in a **Post-Impressionist** style, but having witnessed the 'creation' of Cubism at first hand, Gris was keen to follow the Cubist path. In January 1912 he held his first exhibition at a gallery owned by a dealer called Clovis Sagot. Sagot bought several of the works and Gris gave up his career as an illustrator. In March he contributed three pictures to the **Salon des Indépendants**.

▓ *Juan Gris was not yet twenty when he arrived in Paris from his native Spain, fleeing the obligation on every young Spaniard to serve for a time in the military.*

In the autumn he exhibited with the **Section d'Or**, alongside Léger, Gleizes, Metzinger, Delaunay, the Duchamp brothers and la Fresnaye. Gris also contributed canvases to Cubist exhibitions held at the Galerie Dalmau, Barcelona, Spain and at the Der Sturm gallery in Berlin, Germany. That winter Kahnweiler gave Gris a generous contract to buy all of his future work as well as any work he had in his studio. According to Kahnweiler, it left Gris 'free to paint without ... [financial] worries'.

From the outset, Gris seemed to understand Cubism perfectly. His early works showed an individuality that became a major influence on the development of Cubism. In 1912 he devised a grid structure of criss-cross panels: in each section

■■■ *Homage to Pablo Picasso*, by Juan Gris (1912)
*This is one of three canvases Gris exhibited at the **Salon des Indépendants**. Using the restricted colours of **Analytical Cubism** it shows Picasso sitting cross-legged, holding a paint-splashed palette. Enthusing over this new talent, Apollinaire called Gris' style 'Integral Cubism'.*

he showed the subject from a different viewpoint. Several members of the Section d'Or adopted the grid structure. Gris had a restless and impatiently inventive talent. However, at the end of 1912, he abandoned his grid style and began dividing subjects into long vertical strips.

In August 1913 Gris stayed at Céret, the former monastery in the Pyrenees popular with several artists. It was his first holiday – albeit a working holiday – and he felt comfortable in the relaxed atmosphere in a climate like that of his native Spain. His visit coincided with one by Picasso and they exchanged many ideas before Picasso left suddenly on 15 August. Gris stayed until the autumn and produced many fine works – dispatching them to Kahnweiler as soon as the paint was dry.

In late 1913 Gris began a relationship with a young woman called Charlotte Herpin – better known by her nickname of Josette. They began to live together in 1914, and though they never married, they stayed together as man and wife until Gris' death in 1927. Less than a year after Picasso and Braque's first **collages**, Gris also began gluing wood-grain, labels, newspaper headlines, sheets of music and pages from books to his canvases. Between 1913 and 1915, he completed works of collage that rank alongside those of Picasso and Braque.

In Gris' collages, elements represent what they are: wood-grain represents wood, newsprint a newspaper and so on. In *Violin and Engraving* (1913) he fixed an actual engraving into a picture frame shown in the background. In *The Marble Console* (1914) he added a piece of mirror. 'Surfaces can be recreated and volumes interpreted in a picture, but what is one to do about a mirror whose surface is always changing and which should reflect even the spectator? There is nothing else to do but stick on a real piece.'

When World War I broke out, most of Gris' French colleagues were called up to serve in the French army. Several were wounded. Daniel-Henri Kahnweiler, who was German, was forced into exile. The French government seized his gallery stock. Gris and Josette were staying in Collioure in south-west France. With the coming of war, trains were taken over for military transport, making a return to Paris difficult. Without an income, Gris relied on friends; he and Josette stayed with the parents of a friend from Madrid. Later the artist Henri Matisse joined them in the region. The two men got on well and a friendship grew. (This would later put a strain on Gris' relationship with Picasso – Picasso and Matisse were great rivals.)

In October Gris was finally able to return to Paris. Matisse tried to arrange for several dealers to buy his work, and the writer Gertrude Stein lent him money. Gris, however, was in a difficult position – he still felt bound to his contract with Kahnweiler, even though Kahnweiler was not in a position to help him.

In 1915 Picasso introduced him to a French dealer called Léonce Rosenberg, who agreed to buy his work for the duration of the war.

Like Picasso, Gris did not enlist in the army. As a healthy male who was not in the army and a foreigner, his presence in Paris aroused suspicion. (He could not return to Spain, however, since he had left to avoid conscription.) As the war progressed, public hostility to **avant-garde** art had a particular impact on the foreign non-soldiers, Gris and Picasso. Among the avant-garde there was a demand for a return to tradition – what poet Jean Cocteau later called the 'recall to order'.

The 'recall to order' was a useful discipline for Gris. He kept a low public profile – taking part in fewer exhibitions, for example – and started to link his work to traditional French themes and great works of French art. From September 1916, when Gris accompanied Josette to her hometown of Beaulieu, in the Touraine region, he started to do fewer still lifes and instead completed more figure paintings. Wartime examples include *Woman with a Mandolin after Corot* (1916), *Portrait of Josette Gris* (1916), *Harlequin (after Cézanne)* (1916) and *Harlequin with Guitar* (1917).

In April 1919, after the war had ended, Gris held his first major solo show at Rosenberg's Galerie l'Effort Moderne, in Paris. When Kahnweiler was finally able to return to Paris in 1920, he said of Gris, 'I had left behind a young painter ... I had returned to find a master.' But Gris' art declined dramatically in the 1920s. He was badly affected by a serious chest complaint. At first it was thought to be pneumonia, but developed into pleurisy (an infection of the chest cavity) in 1920 from which he never fully recovered. Designing stage sets and costumes for Diaghilev's Ballets Russes also took up much of his time.

Gris had also aroused the anger of the man he once called 'cher maitre' ('dear master'). Pablo Picasso demanded unquestioning loyalty from his circle, and would become childishly sulky if he did not get it. As Gris' friendship with Matisse developed, Picasso belittled Gris to mutual friends, like Gertrude Stein, and tried to persuade Kahnweiler to stop representing him. In May 1921, Gris was invited to work on a Ballets Russes production called *Cuadro Flamenco*. When he became ill and fell behind with his designs, Picasso stepped in, purely to undermine Gris in the eyes of the Ballets Russes' manager, Diaghilev.

Gris' health continued to worsen. He experienced high blood pressure, and his breathing continued to trouble him. He could still produce work of great quality, but his output was uneven. In 1925 his health deteriorated still further despite frequent visits to the South of France with Josette.

In 1926, Gris was considering taking French citizenship. Family members in Madrid criticized him, but he received a letter from his son, Georges, in which he made it clear he hated life in the Spanish capital as much as his father had. Gris summoned Georges from Madrid. Later that year Gris was diagnosed as suffering from serious asthma and was prescribed morphine to help combat its effects.

Shortly after his 40th birthday in 1927, Gris spoke optimistically of a new way of working: 'I believe that I am approaching a new period of self-expression, of pictorial expression, of picture language: a well thought-out and well blended unity.' Soon after, on 11 May 1927, Juan Gris died.

The Sunblind, by Juan Gris (1914)
*A clever combination of false wood-effect, **collage** and painting, The Sunblind is a typical example of Juan Gris' work between 1913 and 1915. By the end of 1914 colour was playing an increasingly important role in his work.*

Roger de la Fresnaye 1885–1925

- Born 11 July 1885, Le Mans, France.
- Died 27 November 1925, Grasse, France.

Key cubist works
The Italian Girl (1911)
Italian Girl (Bronze sculpture) (1911)
Jeanne d'Arc (1912)
Conquest of the Air (1913)

Roger de la Fresnaye was born in 1885, in the town of Le Mans, in the Sarthe region of north-west France, where his father – a senior army officer – was temporarily stationed. The family came from an aristocratic Norman background, and their home was the Château de la Fresnaye, near Falaise in Normandy, northern France.

La Fresnaye enjoyed a cultured and classical education, as befitted his social background. He decided as a young man that he wanted to study art, his family agreed and provided him with an allowance. He moved to Paris in 1903 and enrolled at the Académie Julian. He then studied at the prestigious **École des Beaux-Arts** until 1908. In 1908 he attended the Académie Ranson.

In 1910 la Fresnaye met Raymond Duchamp-Villon at a sculpture studio in Montparnasse, Paris. Through Duchamp-Villon, he met several Salon Cubists. Their influence was soon obvious in his work, notably in his painting *The Italian Girl* (1911) and several landscapes he completed the following year. Encouraged by Duchamp-Villon, la Fresnaye was also one of the first of the Salon Cubists to explore the possibilities of sculpture. He produced a bronze piece called *Italian Girl* in 1911, based on his own painting.

Over the next year, influenced by new friends and the work of Paul Cézanne, la Fresnaye developed his own Cubist style. He remained faithful to traditional painting techniques, however, and used Cubist ideas to reinterpret traditional scenes, rather than to establish an entirely original and radical Cubist style. His work remained far more 'naturalistic' (more recognizably realistic) and colourful than that of Braque and Picasso, for example. He thought of himself as a painter of contemporary history.

In 1911, la Fresnaye exhibited with his fellow Cubists at the **Salon des Indépendants**, and at a Cubist exhibition in Brussels, Belgium. At the 1911 **Salon d'Automne**, Duchamp-Villon and la Fresnaye were elected onto the hanging committee and conspired to have all Cubist work hung together in one room – Salle 8. There was a repeat of the rumpus that had accompanied the Cubists' scheming at the Salon des Indépendants. One outraged critic wrote that the Cubists had 'an unquenchable thirst for noise and publicity'.

In 1912, la Fresnaye joined the **Section d'Or** and regularly visited the Duchamp brothers' studios. Though often regarded as an unoriginal artist, la Fresnaye made Cubism more accessible to ordinary people and actually did much to popularize the movement and spread its influence before 1914.

La Fresnaye's later works showed the influence of Fernand Léger and Robert Delaunay. The latter, in particular, had a major impact on la Fresnaye's use of colour. By 1913 la Fresnaye had become a devotee of Delaunay's **Orphic Cubism**, or **Orphism**.

La Fresnaye served in the French army during World War I. While in the trenches, he painted portraits of his fellow servicemen. He served for three years, but contracted tuberculosis, a very serious bacterial infection of the lungs. He was invalided out of the army in 1917, still dangerously unwell. For the sake of his health, la Fresnaye moved to Grasse, a town in the mountains of southern France with a very temperate climate. However, he never regained sufficient energy for prolonged work. He produced a number of Cubist watercolours and drawings, but in the last years of his life he abandoned Cubism completely for a more traditional and decorative style of painting and drawing. He died in Grasse, on 27 November 1925.

▌▌▌ *Self-portrait, by Roger de la Fresnaye (c. 1907–08)*
Though best known as a painter, la Fresnaye was one of the first Salon Cubists to explore the possibilities that Cubist ideas presented to sculptors.

Fernand Léger 1881–1955

- Born 4 February 1881, Argentan, Normandy, France.
- Died 17 August 1955, Gif-sur-Yvette, France.

Key cubist works
Woman Sewing (1909)
Study for Three Portraits (1910–11)
Smokers (1911)
The Wedding (1911–12)
Contrast of Forms (1913)
Houses among Trees (1914)
The Card Players (1917)

Fernand Léger was born into a rural family in Argentan, Normandy, and spoke proudly of his Norman roots. He attended the local school and completed his education at a Catholic school in nearby Tinchebray. His father, Henri-Armand Léger, was a cattle merchant with a quarrelsome character. Léger recalled: 'My mother was a saintly woman who spent years of her life making good the damage done by my father.' Fernand's father died when he was young and it was his mother, Marie-Adèle Danou, who brought him up on their farm at Lisores. Though interested in art, at sixteen Léger was sent to work as an apprentice architect in Caen. He remained for two years. The training proved invaluable in his development as an artist.

In 1900, Léger arrived in Paris, aged nineteen. He earned a living in various architect's offices. In 1902–03, he completed his **military service** in the engineers, stationed at Versailles, outside Paris. After finishing, he failed the entrance exams for the **École des Beaux-Arts**, but secured a place at another Paris art school, École des Arts Décoratifs. (He did, however, attend lectures at the École des Beaux-Arts given by one teacher, Léon Gérôme, who opened his lectures to the public.) Léger also enrolled as a student at the Académie Julian and often visited the Louvre museum. When he could afford it, Léger travelled to the island of Corsica to paint. To support himself, he worked as a part-time draughtsman and as a retouching artist in a photographic studio.

Like many artists of his generation, Léger started out emulating the **Impressionists**. In 1907, he visited the Paul Cézanne **retrospective**. His work soon reflected his admiration for Cézanne. (Léger described him as 'the artist of transition between modern painters and Impressionism' and confessed it took him three years to cast off Cézanne's influence.) He was also influenced by **Fauvism**. In 1908 he took a studio in La Ruche where he befriended the sculptors Henri Laurens, Jacques Lipchitz and Alexander Archipenko and in 1909 met Robert Delaunay, Marc Chagall and the poet Guillaume Apollinaire. (He first encountered the work of Picasso and Braque in 1909, on a visit to Daniel-Henri Kahnweiler's gallery.)

By 1909, Léger was committed to taking a new direction – which he recognized as being Cubism. He abandoned the colourful style of Fauvism and began using a limited range of colours. In a dramatic effort to break decisively with his own past he also destroyed almost all his early work. Léger's first Cubist effort was *Woman Sewing* (1909). He showed work at the **Salons d'Automne** of 1909 and 1910. In 1910, after the Salon d'Automne, Albert Gleizes persuaded Léger to associate himself with the Salon Cubists. Léger also sold several pieces to Kahnweiler.

Under the influence of his first encounter with work by Braque in 1909, Léger completed a series of Cubist cityscapes. However, despite the impact of Braque and his subsequent membership of the **Section d'Or**, Léger kept his distance from full-blown Cubism. He often tried to include a sense of movement and vitality that was absent from the works of Braque and Picasso. In *Study for Three Portraits* (1910–11), *Smokers* (1911) and *The Wedding* (1911–12), Léger tried to capture movement by showing a multitude of hands, faces, flashes of colour, plumes of smoke. He had also recognized how the speed of motorized cars, planes and trains had changed the way people saw things. As he later said: 'The window of the [train] ... the windshield of the car ... the speed at which you are travelling, have changed the familiar look of things. Modern man registers one hundred times more impressions than an 18th-century artist.' By 1911, Léger had developed his own Cubist style.

▥ *Léger was tall and heavily built, and always dressed soberly. The brim of the cloth cap he wore in the studio was heavily singed, a consequence of brushing against the stovepipe when he bent to stoke the coals.*

In 1912, Léger held his first one-man exhibition at Kahnweiler's gallery. In 1913, Kahnweiler offered Léger a formal contract to buy his paintings. When Léger's uncle, a legal official who had tried to divert Léger away from art, saw the value of the contract he immediately dropped his opposition! That year Léger moved into a studio on the Rue Notre Dame des Champs in Montparnasse, which remained his home for over 40 years.

■■ *The Wedding* by Fernand Léger (1911–12)
Based on the marriage of a friend, The Wedding *depicts a bridal procession through a crowd. By overlapping geometric shapes and images, merging individuals in the crowd into a single mass and including distant views of buildings, Léger creates a dynamic image full of movement and action.*

André Lhôte 1885–1962

André Lhôte was born in Bordeaux, France in 1885. In 1905 he taught himself to paint and moved to Paris. In 1910 he held his first one-man show at a small gallery in Paris, which brought him into contact with several Salon Cubists, such as Léger. They persuaded him to adopt a much more obviously Cubist style. By 1911 he was exhibiting alongside the Cubists at the **Salon d'Automne**.

Lhôte tackled a range of subjects including landscapes, portraits, still lifes, interiors and mythological scenes. His most famous painting is *Portrait of Marguerite* (1913). He wanted to develop a theory of Cubism through his writings and his role as a teacher. As a consequence he was often referred to as 'the academician of Cubism'. He worked as a critic from 1917 until 1940 and exerted a great influence over many artists through his art school – the Académie Montparnasse – which he opened in 1922.

Kahnweiler's contract gave Léger plenty of room for artistic experimentation. Léger's interest in colour grew, and for a while he was happy to be described as an **Orphist**. This interest in colour led to a series of paintings called *Contrast of Forms* (1913), which are some of the earliest **abstract** paintings ever done and seemed to show the direction he was heading in. That same year he also participated in the New York **Armory Show**, which was the USA's first introduction to European **avant-garde** art. In 1913 and 1914 Léger also began to give public lectures – widely reprinted in France, Germany and Italy – on modern art at the Académie Wassilev, in Paris.

However, in August 1914, Léger was called up to serve in World War I. He served on the Western Front until 1916, first as a sapper – a soldier who digs trenches, fortifications and graves – in the Argonne Forest and later as a stretcher-bearer at Verdun. His experiences both horrified him as a man and inspired him as an artist. They killed any romantic ideas he might have had about the glory of war.

Léger's experiences also radically altered his view of art and its role in society: 'I found myself on an equal footing with the whole of the French people ... my new comrades were miners, labourers, artisans in wood or metal. I discovered the people of France.' In 1915, out of loyalty to his fellow soldiers, he refused the offer of a transfer to the comfort of the French army's camouflage unit. He decided he wanted to create art as tough and accurate as the straight-to-the-point slang of his fellow soldiers. He believed art should respond to the real lives of working people.

Léger was also deeply affected by the terrible beauty of precision engineering and technology: 'I was ... stunned by the sight of the open breech of a 75mm gun in full sunlight, confronted with the play of light on white metal.' He drew every spare minute. Whenever he returned to Paris on leave, he dumped bundles of sketches with his girlfriend, Jeanne Lohy.

■ *Contrasting Forms*, by Fernand Léger (1913)

*For a short period in 1913, Léger completed a series of **abstract**, or non-figurative, experiments called Contrasts of Forms. Made up of geometric shapes and primary colours they showed nothing 'real'. Léger soon abandoned this approach and once again began representing reality in his work.*

Léger was gassed in September 1916. He was shipped to a hospital at Villepinte where he spent over a year **convalescing**. It was here he began to paint again and he completed many canvases before he was finally discharged from the army and the hospital at the end of 1917. In 1919 he and Jeanne Lohy married in Paris.

During the 1920s Léger was involved in many activities, including book illustration, cinema and theatre set design. He also travelled and lectured widely. With the artist Amédée Ozenfant he founded the Académie de l'Art Moderne in Paris, in 1924. He also organized art courses for workers at the Renault car factory. In 1924 he made the experimental film *Ballet Mécanique (Mechanical Ballet)*. Social and political commitments became increasingly important to Léger. Léger's marriage to Jeanne Lohy collapsed in the 1920s. By the 1930s he was deliberately trying to make his work more accessible to people by relating it to popular culture, especially cinema and adverts.

The 1930s were a time of rising tension throughout Europe. Economic depression and unemployment caused great misery, and provoked rising anger on both the left and right. Guided by his left-wing sympathies, Léger joined the **Popular Front**, an alliance between the French Socialist and Communist parties.

In May 1940, during World War II, the Germans invaded France. Léger was staying on his family's farm at Lisores. His politics made him a marked man and Léger fled south, first to Bordeaux and then on to the Mediterranean port of Marseilles. In late October he managed to find passage on a ship sailing to the USA, a country he had visited several times in the 1920s and 1930s. He remained there throughout the war, teaching at Yale University and Mills College, California, taking acrobats and cyclists as his favourite subjects for his painting. He returned to France in 1945, soon after liberation. He immediately threw himself back into political activity, joining the French Communist Party and committing his art to 'the service of the people'. He also reopened his art academy.

While Léger continued to paint, he opened a ceramics studio in 1949 and also worked in mosaic and tapestry. He enjoyed public projects, and in spite of his Communist beliefs, he completed several stained-glass commissions for the Church – for example Audincourt church.

In February 1952, he married Nadia Khodossevich. Nadia had been a student at Léger's Académie de l'Art Moderne in 1924 and had been his assistant for many years. They moved to a new home at Gros Tilleul, in Gif-sur-Yvette.

Léger continued to work until his sudden death from a heart attack at home in 1955.

Jacques Lipchitz 1891–1973

- Born 10 August (22 August, in the New Russian calendar) 1891, Druskininkai, Lithuania, Russian Empire.
- Died 26 May 1973, Capri, Italy.

Key cubist works
Sailor with a Guitar (1914)
Detachable Figure: Dancer (1915)
Man with Guitar (1916)

Jacques Lipchitz was born Chaim Jacob Lipchitz to wealthy Jewish parents in 1891, in Lithuania – then part of the Russian Empire. As a young man, he studied engineering and showed little interest in modern art. However, news of the exciting French **avant-garde** art scene ignited his curiosity. Supported by his family, he moved to Paris in 1909. Initially he studied the art of Ancient Greece, Egypt and Rome.

▓ *Lipchitz was keenly aware of his Jewish heritage. In the 1930s, as the Nazi menace grew, Lipchitz's work, such as* The Rape of Europa, *came to represent the coming conflict.*

Lipchitz enrolled at the **École des Beaux-Arts**. He studied sculpture there for two years, and had his early work praised by the leading French sculptor Auguste Rodin. Lipchitz got married to Berthe and in 1912 moved into La Ruche, taking a studio next to the sculptor Constantin Brancusi. Brancusi, though never a Cubist, encouraged the young Lipchitz.

Lipchitz returned to Russia to do **military service** in the Imperial Russian Army between 1912 and 1913. He fell ill while in the army and was eventually declared unfit to serve. He returned to Paris in 1913 where he met Pablo Picasso. From around 1913, Lipchitz worked as a Cubist. He threw himself into his work and produced sculptures, such as *Sailor with a Guitar* (1914). From 1915, he produced pieces based on the idea of collapsible components, similar to sculptures that Picasso had been working on since 1912.

By the end of World War I, Lipchitz's work became less **abstract**. His favourite objects were musical instruments and they soon became an important part of his sculptures. In 1920 a wealthy American collector called Albert Barnes bought some work from Lipchitz. He also began to commission work. This gave Lipchitz more creative freedom – it meant he could cast sculptures in bronze, which was expensive but much more durable. That same year, he had his first solo exhibition at Léonce Rosenberg's Galerie de l'Effort Moderne.

In 1924 he moved from Paris to Boulogne-sur-Seine and began work on a series of bronze sculptures, collectively known as 'Transparents' or 'Open Sculptures'. In 1928 Lipchitz took French citizenship.

After the German invasion of France in 1940, and anxious to escape the Nazi persecution of Jews, Lipchitz and his wife hid in the southern French city of Toulouse. In 1941 they fled to the USA, where they settled. Lipchitz had an international reputation and, during the 1940s, began producing large, monumental works for public commission.

Lipchitz returned to France after World War II. He and Berthe divorced and he married a sculptor, Yulla. They moved back to the USA in 1946. They had a daughter, Lolya, an event that inspired several pieces exploring motherhood.

In 1952 a fire in Lipchitz's studio destroyed many of his early works and several in progress. This stimulated him to further invention. By 1955 he was producing what he called 'semi-automatic-masses' – pieces of clay he shaped under water using only his sense of touch, which were then cast in bronze.

Lipchitz spent most of his last decade on the isle of Capri, Italy. He continued to work but the effort required to produce large pieces was now too great. Lipchitz died in Capri in May 1973.

▮▮ *Arlequin*, by Jacques Lipchitz (1919)
Musicians and actors, and especially the character of the Harlequin, were taken as subjects by most of the major Cubist artists. Though Lipchitz was gradually moving away from Cubism, this 1919 piece clearly shows a strong Cubist influence.

Jean Metzinger 1883–1956

- Born 24 June 1883, in Nantes, France.
- Died 3 November 1956, in Paris, France.

Key cubist works
Cubist Landscape (1911)
Le Goûter (Tea-Time) (1911)
Portrait of Gleizes (1912)
Dancer in a Café (1912)
Head of a Woman in a Hat (1912)
Still Life (1917)

Portrait of Jean Metzinger, by Suzanne Phocas (1926)
An acquaintance of Picasso and Braque and the Salon Cubists, Jean Metzinger linked the secretive development of Montmartre Cubism with the much more public development of Salon Cubism.

Jean Metzinger was born into a wealthy family in Nantes, France, in 1883. Though a keen artist, he studied medicine in his home town and painted only as a hobby. However, favourable reviews of his work at the 1903 **Salon des Indépendants** persuaded him to abandon his studies and pursue an artistic career. Metzinger moved to Paris in 1905, and met Robert Delaunay. They shared an interest in **Neo-Impressionism** and often painted together. Metzinger exhibited regularly at the Salon exhibitions and from 1906 he was a member of the hanging committee of the Salon des Indépendants.

Metzinger exhibited with Picasso and Braque at Wilhelm Uhde's gallery in 1908. Picasso was a significant influence on Metzinger for several years, and Metzinger was closer in style to Picasso and Braque than any other artists.

Metzinger persuaded the other artists who became known as Cubists that they were united in a common purpose – to reform painting. The five artists who had exhibited at the 1910 Salon des Indépendants – Metzinger, Gleizes, Delaunay, Léger and le Fauconnier – exhibited again at the 1910 **Salon d'Automne**. Metzinger persuaded a friendly writer and critic called Roger Allard to review their works on display. Allard's article talked, for the first time, about an art that was trying to analyse objects rather than simply reproduce them.

Soon after the Salon d'Automne, Metzinger wrote an article himself called 'A Note on Painting'. In it he linked the work of Picasso and Braque with the efforts of Delaunay, Gleizes, Léger and the rest. He also tried to claim that

Cubism represented a 'new classicism' – by which he meant it was not a break with the past, but was in fact closely connected to classical, and especially French classical, art. Metzinger also tried to raise the credibility of the Salon Cubists, who had been accused by Apollinaire of stealing Picasso's ideas.

Metzinger played a leading role in rigging the infamous Salon des Indépendants of 1911 (see page 7). Apollinaire reviewed the exhibition, and while praising what he saw in Salle 41, he singled Metzinger out as the only true Cubist among the artists exhibiting at the Salon.

In 1911 Metzinger met the Duchamp brothers. In 1912 he showed *Portrait of Gleizes* at the **Section d'Or** exhibition. In the same year, Metzinger and Gleizes wrote the book *Du 'Cubisme' (On 'Cubism')*. It was the first theoretical explanation of Cubism and became very influential.

Metzinger fought in World War I but was discharged in 1915. He exhibited in New York with Marcel Duchamp and Albert Gleizes at the Montross Gallery in 1916. In 1919 he returned to Paris, where he remained for the rest of his life. During the 1920s he abandoned Cubism and adopted a more realistic style of painting, partly inspired by Fernand Léger. However, several works he completed in the 1940s showed a partial return to Cubism. He remained an important figure in French art until his death in 1956 in Paris, France.

▊▊ *Dancer in a Café*, by Jean Metzinger (1912)
Dancer in a Café is a good example of the way Metzinger tried to connect his modern techniques and subjects with classic, long-established themes, in this case, the modern fashions of the dancer with the traditional structure of the painting.

Francis Picabia 1879–1953

- Born 22 January 1879, Paris, France.
- Died 30 November 1953, Paris, France.

Key cubist works

Dances at the Spring I (1912)
Dances at the Spring II (1912)
Procession in Seville (1912)
Udnie (Young American Girl: Dance) (1913)
Edtaonisl (Ecclesiastic) (1913)
I See Again in Memory My Dear Udnie (1914)
Parade Amoureuse (Love Parade) (1917)

Francis Picabia was born François Marie Martinez Picabia, the son of a Cuban diplomat father and a French mother, who left him wealthy enough to follow his artistic instincts without having to earn a living. He grew up in Paris and nursed artistic ambitions. He studied at both the **École des Beaux-Arts** and at the École des Arts Décoratifs. He also studied for a time under the great **Impressionist** painter Camille Pissarro.

Picabia invented many outrageous stories about his youth. He claimed that, at sixteen, he had run away to Switzerland with an older woman, where he met the German philosopher Friedrich Nietzsche. Whether this meeting ever happened, Nietzsche's philosophy of the '*Ubermensch*' – the Superman who acts according to his own laws rather than the conventions of society – was certainly an influence on Picabia. Picabia also had a lifelong obsession with machinery – owning scores of cars and at least a dozen yachts – which had a huge impact on his art. He dreamed of the creation of a perfect human-mechanical hybrid, a superman.

Picabia moved rapidly through several styles of painting. In 1903 he exhibited work inspired by the Impressionists at the **Salon d'Automne** and the **Salon des Indépendants**. He held his first solo show in 1905. By 1908, the biggest influence on Picabia's work was the vibrant and colourful art of the **Fauvists** and the otherworldly art of the **Symbolists**. In 1909, he began to take an interest in Cubist developments.

Early in 1912 Picabia married Gabrielle Buffet. The couple's honeymoon provided the inspiration for several of Picabia's paintings, including *Dances at the Spring I* (1912) and *Dances at the Spring II* (1912), both created using Cubist techniques. Picabia was later a founder member of the **Section d'Or**.

In June 1912 Picabia showed work at an exhibition in the Normandy town of Rouen, largely organized by the Duchamp brothers. It was the first time that Picabia had actually exhibited alongside the Cubists.

Picabia exhibited *Dances at the Spring I* at the Salon d'Automne of 1912, alongside several members of the Section d'Or. In October 1912, Picabia and Gabrielle, Apollinaire and Duchamp took a driving holiday to the Jura Mountains. For the two artists it was more than just a holiday. It was, Gabrielle recalled, a trip into 'witticism and clownery ... the disintegration ... of art'. Both Picabia and Duchamp began to develop their ideas in a direction that would eventually take them beyond Cubism.

In February 1913, Picabia travelled to the USA for the **Armory Show**. He was the only European artist exhibiting who could actually afford to go. He also exhibited at the 291 Gallery in New York, run by Alfred Stieglitz, a photographer and art dealer. Stieglitz was committed to bringing modern European art to the attention of the American public. Picabia published the first of his 'machine drawings' in Stieglitz's magazine *Camera Work*.

▌▌ *Francis Picabia*, by Paul Dermée (1920)
Picabia was an extraordinary individual and artist. He completed several well-received landscapes in a style influenced by the Impressionist painter Alfred Sisley but, typically, adopted a series of contemporary styles in quick succession, including Symbolism, **Neo-Impressionism** *and Fauvism.*

Because Picabia used such bright colours and was moving towards a more **abstract** form of Cubism, Apollinaire identified him with **Orphic Cubism**. Typical pieces of work included *Udnie (Young American Girl: Dance)* (1913) and a companion piece, *Edtaonisl (Ecclesiastic)* (1913). Both were criticized at the Salon d'Automne of 1913, but Picabia did not care. He explained them as 'memories of America' – inspired by his time in New York. In fact *Udnie* and another painting called *I See Again in Memory My Dear Udnie* (1914) were based on a short affair Picabia had during a transatlantic voyage with a ballet dancer called Udnie Napierkowska.

Picabia was conscripted into the French army in 1914. In 1915, he was given money and sent to negotiate the purchase of molasses from Cuba. Instead he returned to the USA, linking up with Marcel Duchamp and several other artists including the painter and photographer Man Ray. His interest in machinery and automation was growing and he believed that he could combine art and technology.

Picabia was soon involved in **Dadaist** art and contributed to a periodical published by Stieglitz called *291*. European Dadaism had a political element – the Dadaists believed art and artists had been irrevocably changed by the slaughter of World War I. They also rejected the nationalism and materialism they believed had caused the war in the first place. Picabia and the New York Dadaists were less concerned about the war and much more aggressive towards the art establishment – in which they now included even as revolutionary an art as Cubism. It had become 'respectable' and the artists were smug, self-satisfied members of the art establishment. Art had a job to do – to shock people out of their complacency.

■■ *Procession in Seville*, by Francis Picabia (1912)
Procession in Seville *is based on a sinister column of hooded penitents Picabia saw marching through the southern Spanish city of Seville during the Easter Semana Santa (Holy Week).*

Despite his wealth, Picabia was a natural rebel. He abandoned traditional art and the **avant-garde**, which he believed had become traditional, and became the sworn enemy of Cubism. (Famously he once exhibited a stuffed monkey labelled *Portrait of Cézanne, Portrait of Rembrandt, Portrait of Renoir*.) Picabia returned to Europe at the end of 1916. He settled in Barcelona, Spain, to recover from the excesses of opium and alcohol consumption. The following January he founded a Dadaist periodical called *391*, in homage to Stieglitz's *291*. He returned to the USA later that year where he continued to publish *391*, assisted by Marcel Duchamp.

After a year in Switzerland he returned to Paris, and used *391* to attack the **Salon d'Automne** for 'hiding' his 'biological-machine' painting *Child Carburettor* (1919). This controversy put him at the head of the new Paris Dadaist movement. Though a sworn enemy of the Cubists, he often used Cubist techniques such as **collage** in his work. Because Dadaism was very confrontational, it could not last. Picabia sided with André Breton against several other Dadaist artists. In 1923, Breton split the movement during a Dadaist event that ended in violence. Breton went on to establish **Surrealism** in 1924. Picabia himself denounced Dadaism as no longer being 'new'.

Though one Surrealist dismissed Picabia as 'already the past', Picabia experimented with Surrealism for many years. Dada was dead, he claimed, and Surrealism its successor. In 1923, he moved to Tremblay-sur-Mauldre, outside Paris, and returned to a more figurative art – one based on recognizable subjects. In 1924 he attacked Breton and the Surrealists in his magazine *391*. From 1924 until 1936, Picabia lived in the South of France. He owned a house in the shape of a tower and on top he had a racing car fixed to a huge radial arm so that he could speed round and round, looking at the landscape flash by! His work grew increasingly **abstract**.

During World War II, Picabia lived in North Africa and Spain. He was cut off from most of his contemporaries and for a while his work became very conventional. He returned to Paris in 1947. Re-establishing old friendships, he began to paint with renewed passion. His wife Gabrielle said 'he gave himself totally to painting'. In 1949 a **retrospective** exhibition was organized in Paris. The catalogue for the exhibition, titled *491*, contained articles by Breton and Jean Cocteau, amongst others.

In 1951 Picabia was made an Officer of the Légion d'Honneur. He died in Paris in 1953.

Pablo Picasso 1881–1973

- Born 25 October 1881, in Málaga, Andalucia, Spain.
- Died 8 April 1973, in Mougins, France.

Key cubist works

Portrait of Gertrude Stein (1905–06)
Les Demoiselles d'Avignon (1907)
Portrait of Ambroise Vollard (1910)
Bowl with Fruit, Violin and Wineglass (1912–13)
Harlequin (1918)
Three Musicians (1921)
The Three Dancers (1925)

He was born Pablo Ruiz y Picasso in dramatic style. The midwife, believing Picasso was stillborn, put him down to attend to his mother. Picasso's uncle promptly blew a lungful of cigar smoke into the infant's face. With an angry shriek, Picasso took his first breath.

Picasso's father, Don José Ruiz, was a museum curator and painter, who taught drawing in Málaga, Spain. His mother was Maria Picasso López. Before he could speak Picasso used drawings to make people understand his wishes and his first word was '*Piz!*' for *lapis* – pencil. In 1888, tutored by his father, Picasso began to paint.

■■ *Picasso and Fernande Olivier shared a dilapidated building in Montmartre, nicknamed the Bateau Lavoir (Laundry Boat). It became a magnet for a brilliant circle of friends. Picasso put up a sign, 'The Poets' Rendezvous' and later remembered these days as his 'golden age'.*

In 1891 the family moved to La Coruña, Spain, where Don José taught at the School of Fine Arts. In 1892, Picasso was accepted as a student. Though only ten years old, he chose adult subjects: portraits and landscapes. In 1895, Don José took a job at the Barcelona School of Fine Arts. He wanted Pablo admitted as a senior student. Candidates normally had a month to complete the entrance exam – Picasso claimed he completed it in one day!

In 1900, shortly before his nineteenth birthday, Picasso visited Paris. He alternated between Paris and Spain for several years. Isolated and depressed, particularly after the suicide of his close friend Carlos Casagemas in 1901,

Picasso expressed his solitude in pervasive blue tones in his paintings. His subjects were mostly victims. This was known as his 'Blue Period'.

In 1904 Picasso settled permanently in Paris. He met a beautiful, intelligent young woman called Fernande Olivier. With Fernande he found domestic calm. His work took on a pink hue: this became known as the 'Rose Period'. During his Rose Period, two works stand out – *Portrait of Gertrude Stein* and *Self-portrait with Palette*. Both show the influence of 'primitive art' and indicated the direction Picasso was about to take. Ancient European artefacts and masks and statuettes from Africa, Latin America and the Pacific Islands fascinated Picasso. He began making sketches that led to *Les Demoiselles d'Avignon* (1907), a painting many writers believe launched Cubism.

While Picasso's new friend Georges Braque was in L'Estaque in the summer of 1908, Picasso made a visit to the village of La Rue des Bois, on the Oise River near Paris. Here he completed several pictures very similar in style to those Braque was doing.

From 1909, Picasso and Braque worked closely with each other. Braque began to concentrate on still lifes and landscapes, while Picasso focused on figure paintings. In the summer of 1909, inspired by Braque's Cubist landscapes of L'Estaque, Picasso spent the summer at Horta del Ebro, a mountain village in Catalonia, Spain, where he completed his own Cubist landscapes. It was not all he did. In fact, Picasso actually spent most of his time painting a number of Cubist head and shoulders portraits loosely based on Fernande. On his return to Paris, Picasso used *Woman with Pears (Fernande)* (1909) as the basis for a sculpture cast in bronze – *Head of Fernande* (1909). This was the first truly Cubist sculpture.

After showing his 1908–09 work at the gallery of Wilhelm Uhde, Picasso travelled to Cadaqués, a small port on the Catalan coast of Spain. Though an increasing number of artists were using Cubist ideas, and were steadily taking Cubism to the public, Picasso and Braque adopted a low profile in Paris, keeping to themselves and their immediate circle. They only exhibited in selected art galleries, such as those of Daniel-Henri Kahnweiler, Uhde and Ambroise Vollard. It was a strategy that worked. An air of mystery surrounded them and their art, supported by rumour and the word of the art critics. Picasso also exhibited in Munich and London and, the following year, in New York.

By 1911 Picasso and Braque were working so closely together it is difficult to tell which artist did which work. Fernande and Pablo Picasso spent the summer in Céret, a former monastery in the Pyrenean mountains. Braque joined them. Picasso and Braque introduced lettering, snatches of song lyrics, parts of advertising posters and newspaper headlines into their pictures.

These, according to Kahnweiler, were an attempt to introduce 'real' details into the works, to suggest memories in the mind of the viewer and so conjure up the landscape or still life subject. The year 1911 was the highpoint of **Analytical Cubism** and of Picasso's artistic partnership with Braque.

That year, Picasso's relationship with Fernande began to disintegrate. He started an affair with Marcelle Humbert (real name Eve Gouel). Picasso renamed her 'Eva', and celebrated her in Cubist works, such as *Ma Jolie*, which used snatches of song lyrics. In 1912, when Fernande fell for an Italian painter, Picasso seized his moment and lured Marcelle away from her lover, Louis Marcoussis. The pair fled to Céret. Though a creative period, Picasso missed Braque and was pleased when Braque and his wife visited.

In 1912, Picasso and Braque introduced new elements into their art. It was the start of **Synthetic Cubism**. Instead of breaking subjects down and analysing them, they began to reassemble subjects, using simplified shapes and bright colours. After Braque, Picasso also began to experiment with **collage**. He began to collect interestingly patterned wallpapers, newspapers and sheet music.

He also began to create 'constructions' – sculptures made of card, wire and wood that were like three-dimensional collages. After seeing paper constructions by Braque, Picasso made *Guitar* from sheet metal and wire. A critic asked, 'What is it?' Picasso replied, 'I call it a guitar.' That year, Picasso signed an exclusive contract with Kahnweiler. Picasso was now a very wealthy man. He spent much of 1913 in Barcelona and Céret until August, when he returned to Paris.

Portrait of Ambroise Vollard, Pablo Picasso (1910)
Picasso's portrait of the art dealer Ambroise Vollard is a striking example of a Cubist portrait – a multi-faceted analysis of the sitter who is in many ways scarcely recognizable.

Louis Marcoussis 1878–1941

Polish-born Louis Markus arrived in Paris in 1903. He painted in an **Impressionist** style but abandoned painting in 1907 and worked as a cartoonist. In 1910 he met Apollinaire, who persuaded him to change his name to Marcoussis after a village near Paris and also introduced him to Picasso – who promptly seduced away Marcoussis' lover, Marcelle Humbert. In 1911 Marcoussis took up painting again and launched straight into Cubism. He exhibited with the **Section d'Or** in 1912 and 1920. A sensitive and gifted artist, he was not prolific. His strongest influence seems to have been Juan Gris. He was also an etcher and book illustrator.

He and Braque continued to exchange ideas until June 1914. However, in August, World War I began. As a Spanish citizen, Picasso was not conscripted. Meanwhile Eva's health deteriorated. Frightened Picasso would leave her, she kept it secret. When she finally revealed she had tuberculosis, the hypochondriac Picasso fled to his old studio in Bateau Lavoir. Marcelle 'Eva' Humbert died in December 1915. Picasso's dealer, Kahnweiler, then in exile, actually blamed Picasso for stealing her from the protection of Louis Marcoussis.

In 1917 Picasso designed sets and costumes for Jean Cocteau's *Parade*, performed by the Ballets Russes. Picasso's designs were a shocking departure from traditional sets. Apollinaire described *Parade* as 'surrealist' – the first use of the word. However, there were already changes in Picasso's revolutionary and confrontational style. Though he continued to produce Cubist works, from 1916 he adopted a more conventional style of painting that was classical in its inspiration, accepting the demand that during the war there should be a 'recall to order' in art and culture.

Picasso met Olga Koklova, a dancer with the Ballets Russes and they married in 1918. She was of an aristocratic Russian family and had very **conservative** values, which she tried to impose on Picasso. When he painted her she said: 'I want to recognize my face.' They moved into a grand apartment and Picasso seemed to settle down. The birth of his first child, Paul, followed in 1921.

While Picasso enjoyed the life of high society many of his friends were angered. Juan Gris wrote to Kahnweiler, 'Picasso still does good things, when he finds time between a Russian ballet and a society portrait.' Braque, too, raged against Picasso's surrender to the good life.

By 1925 Picasso was being drawn towards **Surrealism**. He joined the Surrealists' first exhibition but realized his artistic freedom depended on not being labelled and kept his distance. In 1927 Picasso met a young woman called Marie-Thérèse Walter. Struck by her beauty, Picasso persuaded her to sit for him and he produced many famous pictures of her. (They soon became lovers.)

In the early 1930s there were major **retrospectives** of Picasso's work in Paris, Barcelona and Switzerland. He was the most respected artist of the age. In 1935 he and Olga separated. Marie-Thérèse Walter bore him a daughter that same year – María de la Concepción – known as Maya.

Returning to Paris from a holiday in July 1936, Picasso learned of the outbreak of the Spanish Civil War. Dora Maar, his new lover, encouraged him to express support for the legitimate Spanish government.

When the Spanish Republic fell in 1939, Picasso could no longer return to the land of his birth. Then the Germans invaded France in 1940 and Picasso found himself isolated in Paris. He retreated into his Parisian studio, which also became his living accommodation. While not openly political, Picasso refused invitations of refuge in other countries and his presence in Paris was significant to many French citizens. The Germans did not harass Picasso. Though labelled the foremost exponent of '**degenerate** art', many German officers wanted to buy his paintings!

Bottle Vieux Marc, Glass and Paper, by Pablo Picasso (1913)
*From 1912, Picasso and Braque introduced new elements into their art. Picasso used materials from everyday life in his paintings. He filled his **collages** with puns and jokes, pictures cut from magazines and shreds of newspapers, faux-bois (false wood) effects, paint and charcoal.*

In 1947 Picasso and his new lover Françoise Gilot moved to Vallauris, on the French Riviera. They lived in a small, humble house called La Galloise, which lacked a telephone and only had basic facilities. The town had been a centre of pottery making but was in decline. Picasso revived the ceramics trade with a period of furious production, creating 2000 pieces of pottery in one year!

Picasso and Françoise Gilot had two children, Claude and Paloma. When the relationship ended, Picasso met Jacqueline Roque. He and Jacqueline moved several times as he gradually retreated from public life. However, despite his age, Picasso showed no sign of tiring. Even in his 70s and 80s, Picasso produced hundreds of pieces a year. He died on 8 April 1973 at his villa in Mougins.

▐▌▐ *Three Musicians*, by Pablo Picasso (1921)
Three Musicians is often seen as Picasso's last Cubist painting. The three figures represent Picasso, Apollinaire – who had died in 1918 – and the poet Max Jacob. It represents the passing of Picasso's happy-go-lucky pre-war days.

The Next Generation

Though the 'Cubist Epoch' lasted a very short time and virtually ended in 1914 with the outbreak of World War I, its impact on the development of modern art was profound and long-lasting. One of the earliest movements to be inspired by Cubism was Italian Futurism. It existed alongside Cubism and, though a short-lived artistic movement, it was very dynamic and exciting, and attracted many artists. It quickly exerted an influence on the development of Cubism itself. The Futurists adapted Cubist ideas and techniques to create dynamic images full of movement and speed.

Umberto Boccioni 1882–1916

Umberto Boccioni was born in October 1882 in Reggio, Calabria, Italy. In 1901 while studying at the Academia di Belle Arti in Rome, he met the artist Gino Severini. By 1910, together with several other artists, they began to work under the Futurist name. In 1911 the Futurists, on a visit to Paris, met Pablo Picasso.

By 1912 Boccioni was mainly producing sculptures, although he continued to paint. However, in 1915, Boccioni joined the army. He suffered an accident during training and died on 17 August 1916.

▐▐▐ *The Charge of the Lancers,* by Umberto Boccioni (1915)
Futurists celebrated the violence and speed of the modern world, and wanted to capture this movement and noise in their work. Boccioni was a leading Futurist, but died in the army, before his ideas could be realized.

Cubism also had a huge impact beyond the realms of painting and sculpture, on everything from architecture to fashion design. Cubist patterns were even adapted for use as camouflage on tanks, ships and soldiers' uniforms. In less than ten years, Cubist ideas and innovations changed the way we respond to and try to record the world around us.

Paul Klee 1879–1940

Paul Klee was born in Munchenbuchsee, near Bern in Switzerland. He was an influential artist in the **Expressionist** movement in Germany, contributing seventeen works to the *Blaue Reiter* exhibition in 1912. That same year he visited Robert and Sonia Delaunay in Paris and also saw work by other Cubists. The Delaunay's theories on colour were of particular interest to Klee. He translated an essay on light by Robert Delaunay into German in 1913. By 1914 his work clearly showed the influence of Delaunay.

In 1931 he began to teach at the Düsseldorf Academy, but was sacked in 1933, when the Nazis took power in Germany. He emigrated to Bern in Switzerland, and continued to paint despite declining health. He died in 1940.

Marcel Duchamp 1887–1968

Marcel Duchamp, brother of Raymond Duchamp-Villon, proved to be one of the 20th century's most radical and controversial artists. He studied at the Académie Julian between 1904 and 1905 and then adopted a variety of **avant-garde** styles before he encountered Cubism and Futurism. He was a member of the **Section d'Or** and was particularly interested in depicting the passage of time.

By the time Duchamp arrived in New York in 1915, he was a celebrity. Around the same time he stopped painting, (he only completed one more painting in his life, in 1918) and began to develop, along with Picabia and Apollinaire, an attack on the idea of 'art' that would result in the development of **Dadaist** ideas and in his production of his so-called 'ready-mades'. These were everyday objects he renamed. They were intended to undermine the notion of 'originality' and artistic 'invention'. His most famous ready-made was a urinal entitled *Fountain* (1917). He died in Paris in October 1968. His gravestone reads, 'But it's always other people who die.'

Timeline

1876 Raymond Duchamp-Villon born 5 November

1879 Francis Picabia born 22 January

1881 Albert Gleizes born 8 December; Fernand Léger born 4 February; Pablo Picasso born 25 October

1882 Georges Braque born 13 May

1883 Jean Metzinger born 24 June

1885 Robert Delaunay born 12 April; Sonia Delaunay-Terk born 14 November; Roger de la Fresnaye born 11 July

1887 Alexander Archipenko born 30 May; Juan Gris born 23 March

1891 Jacques Lipchitz born 10 August

1907 Braque exhibits six paintings at **Salon des Indépendants** and sells them all; Picasso completes *Les Demoiselles d'Avignon*

1910 Robert Delaunay and Sonia Terk marry

1911 Picasso and Braque work together in Céret; Metzinger plays a leading role in rigging the hanging of Cubist works at the Salon des Indépendants

1912 Archipenko opens his own art school in Paris; Gleizes and Metzinger publish *Du 'Cubisme'* (*On 'Cubism'*); founding of the **Section d'Or**

1914 Outbreak of World War I – many artists conscripted

1918 End of World War I

1922 Room devoted to Braque at **Salon d'Automne**

1923 Archipenko establishes L'École d'Art in New York

1924 Archipenko invents the Archipentura

1925 Léger makes experimental film *Ballet Mécanique* (*Mechanical Ballet*)

1937 Braque wins Carnegie Prize

1939 Outbreak of World War II

1940 Germans invade France

1945 End of World War II

1961 Braque becomes first living artist to have works exhibited in the Louvre

1964 Sonia Delaunay-Terk becomes first woman to exhibit at the Louvre in her own lifetime

Glossary

abstract describes art that is not based on any existing figure

Analytical Cubism reduction of a subject to its component parts

anti-Semitism person who hates or acts against people because they are Jewish

Armory Show international exhibition of modern art, held in 1913 in New York City. Exhibiting work by many of Europe's leading contemporary artists, the Armory Show marked the beginning of interest in progressive art in the USA.

avant-garde pioneers or innovators in any sphere of the arts

collage pasted-paper picture

conservative describes someone who conforms to strict social rules, is wary of change and holds cautious, moderate views

convalesce to recover from illness or injury

Dadaism violent, provocative and anarchic art that mirrored the disillusionment many young artists felt with World War I

degenerate people and ideas that fell outside the narrow vision of the Nazis

École des Beaux-Arts (School of Fine Arts) official art school financed and run by the French government. The teaching was very conservative.

Expressionism art in which naturalism and traditional ideas are abandoned in favour of an expressive exaggeration and distortion

Fauvism Expressionist style of painting inspired by the Neo-Impressionists and Cézanne, based on intense and vivid colours. The name, meaning 'wild beasts', was coined by a hostile critic in 1905.

Franco-Prussian War war between Prussia and France 1870–71 that inflicted crushing defeats on France and resulted in a humiliating peace at the Treaty of Frankfurt

Impressionism modern art movement started in France in the late 1860s. The Impressionists attempted to capture 'real life' and rejected the dark tones and subjects of academic French painting.

military service obligatory duty for all young Frenchmen to serve in the French military for between one and three years

motif dominant feature or dominant idea of an artistic composition

Neo-Impressionism term used to describe a movement that grew out of Impressionism, fundamentally concerned with light and colour but based on scientific principles

Orphism, or **Orphic Cubism** style evolved from Cubism that tried to create colour harmonies in the fashion of musical harmonies. In its pure use of colour it was an important forerunner of entirely abstract, non-figurative art.

perspective method of representing three dimensions on a two-dimensional surface

Popular Front alliance of Communists and Socialists that contested and won the 1936 elections in France

Post-Impressionism imprecise term used to cover the progressive developments in French painting after the Impressionists

religious icons religious paintings, particularly popular in Russian and eastern European churches

Renaissance (literally 'rebirth') time of incredible artistic and scientific development in 14th-century Italy based on the rediscovery of ancient Greek and Roman art, and scientific and mathematical writings. It laid down the rules that dominated western art for 500 years.

republican follower of a system of government that relies on elected heads of state rather than a monarch

retrospective an exhibition which shows an artist's work from its beginnings to the most recent

Russian Revolution revolutionary takeover of power in 1917 that ended the rule of the Russian royal family and put in place a Communist government under Vladimir Lenin

Salon d'Automne annual exhibition of art founded in 1903 by several artists as a more liberal and open-minded alternative to the official, and conservative, Salon de la Société des Artistes Français

Salon des Indépendants annual exhibition of art open to any artist willing to pay a fee to exhibit. It had no jury and awarded no prizes and was founded by several Post-Impressionist artists in 1884.

Section d'Or exhibition held in 1912 by several Salon Cubists who met regularly at the studio Raymond Duchamp-Villon shared with his brothers in Puteaux and who linked Cubism to the advances in technology that were currently happening

Simultaneity a philosopher called Henri Bergson argued there is 'simultaneous' time active in our minds, where past, present and future coexist. The past exists as memories and the future exists because we look forward to it. Bergson called this coexistence 'simultaneity'. Cubism was linked to Bergson's ideas as it showed the three dimensions of space – height, depth and width – as well as the fourth dimension – time – as past, present and future.

Surrealism aartistic movement based on the absurd, heightened and distorted reality, dreams and the work of the psychiatrist Sigmund Freud

Symbolism art of a loosely organized group of artists in late 19th-century France. It arose in reaction to the naturalism and realism of the Impressionists, and was dedicated to giving visual expression to the mystical, the occult and the emotional.

Synthetic Cubism introduced brighter colours, collage, stencilled lettering and the wood-grain effect called faux bois (false wood) to create objects

Resources

List of famous cubist works

Alexander Archipenko (1887–1964)
Médrano I (Juggler), 1912–13
Médrano II (Dancer), 1913, Solomon Guggenheim Museum, New York, USA
Head: Construction of Crossing Planes, 1913, Perls Galleries, New York, USA
Woman with Fan, 1914 Collection of the Latner Family, Toronto, Canada

Georges Braque (1882–1963)
Large Nude, 1908, Galerie Alex Maguy, Paris, France
Houses at L'Estaque, 1908, Kunstmuseum, Bern, Switzerland
Viaduct at L'Estaque, 1908, Musée National d'Art Moderne, Paris, France
Harbour in Normandy, 1909, The Art Institute of Chicago, Illinois, USA
Castle at La Roche-Guyon, 1909, Stedelijk van Abbe Museum,
Eindhoven, Holland
The Portuguese, 1911, Kunstmuseum, Basel, Switzerland
Fruit Dish and Glass, 1912, Private Collection
Fruit Dish, Ace of Clubs, 1913, Musée National d'Art Moderne, Paris, France

Robert Delaunay (1885–1941)
The Eiffel Tower, 1909–12, canvases from the series can be seen in Museum
Folkwang, Essen, Germany; Solomon R Guggenheim Museum, New York, USA;
the Museum of Modern Art, New York, USA; the Kunstsammlung Nordrhein-
Westfalen, Dusseldorf, Germany
The Windows, 1912–14, canvases from the series can be seen in Solomon R
Guggenheim Museum, New York, USA; Tate Modern, London; Kunsthalle,
Hamburg, Germany
Sun, Tower, Aeroplane: Simultaneous, 1913, Albright-Knox Art Gallery, Buffalo,
New York, USA

Sonia Delaunay-Terk (1885–1979)
Blanket, 1911
Bal Bullier, 1912–13
Three Studies for the Electric Prisms, 1914
Marketplace at Minho, 1915

Raymond Duchamp-Villon (1876–1918)
Baudelaire, 1911, Musée des Beaux-Arts, Rouen, France
The Lovers, 1913, The Latner Family, Toronto, Canada
Seated Woman, 1914, Solomon R Guggenheim Museum, New York, USA
Small Horse, 1914, Edgar Kaufmann Jr. New York
Great Horse, 1914, Musée National d'Art Moderne, Paris, France

Albert Gleizes (1881–1953)

Landscape, 1911, Solomon R Guggenheim Museum, New York, USA
Woman in a Kitchen, 1911, Marlborough Galleries, New York, USA
Harvest Threshing, 1912, Solomon R Guggenheim Museum, New York, USA
The Bathers, 1912, Musée d'Art Moderne de la Ville de Paris, Paris
The Football Players, 1912–13, National Gallery of Art, Washington DC, USA
Landscape at Toul, 1913, Columbus Gallery of Fine Arts
Portrait of Stravinsky, 1914, Private Collection

Juan Gris (1887–1927)

Homage to Pablo Picasso, 1912, The Art Institute of Chicago, Chicago, USA
Man in a Café, 1912, Philadelphia Museum of Art, Philadelphia, USA
The Watch, 1912, Private Collection
The Sunblind, 1914, Tate Modern, London
Still Life before an Open Window: Place Ravignon, 1915, Philadelphia Museum of Art, Philadelphia, USA
Woman with a Mandolin after Corot, 1916, Kunstmuseum, Basel, Switzerland
Portrait of Josette Gris, 1916, Prado Museum, Madrid, Spain
Harlequin with Guitar, 1917, Private Collection

Roger de la Fresnaye (1885–1925)

The Italian Girl, 1911
Italian Girl (Bronze sculpture), 1911, Joseph H Hirshhorn Collection, New York, USA
Bathers, 1912, Nathan Cummings Collection, New York, USA
Marie Ressort with her Cows, 1912–13, Albright-Knox Art Gallery, Buffalo, New York, USA

Fernand Léger (1881–1955)

Woman Sewing, 1909, Musée National d'Art Moderne, Paris, France
Les Nus dans la Forêt, 1909–10, Kroller-Muller Foundation, Otterlo, Holland
Study for Three Portraits, 1910–11, Milwaukee Art Centre, Milwaukee, USA
Smokers, 1911, Solomon R Guggenheim Museum, New York, USA
The Wedding, 1911–12, Musée National d'Art Moderne, Paris, France
Woman in Blue, 1912, Kunstmuseum, Basel, Switzerland
Contrast of Forms, 1913, The Museum of Modern Art, New York, USA
The Card Players, 1917, Kroller-Muller Foundation, Otterlo, Holland

Jacques Lipchitz (1891–1973)

Detachable Figure: Dancer, 1915, Cleveland Museum of Art, Mass. USA
Head, 1915, Tate Modern, London
Seated Figure, 1916, Scottish National Gallery of Art, Edinburgh
Guitar Player, 1918, Stadt Kunstmuseum, Duisberg, Germany

Jean Metzinger (1883–1956)

Cubist Landscape, 1911, Sidney Janis Gallery, New York, USA
Le Goûter (Tea-Time), 1911, Philadelphia Museum of Art,
Philadelphia PA, USA
Dancer in a Café, 1912, Albright-Knox Art Gallery, Buffalo, NY, USA
Still Life, 1917, Metropolitan Museum of Art, New York, USA

Francis Picabia (1879–1953)

Dances at the Spring II ,1912 Museum of Modern Art, New York, USA
Procession in Seville, 1912 Private Collection
Udnie (Young American Girl: Dance), 1913 Musée National d'Art
Moderne, Paris
Parade Amoureuse, 1917 Private Collection

Pablo Picasso (1881–1973)

Portrait of Gertrude Stein, 1905–06, Metropolitan Museum of Art,
New York, USA
Les Demoiselles d'Avignon, 1907, Metropolitan Museum of Art,
New York, USA
Portrait of Ambroise Vollard, 1910, Pushkin Museum, Moscow, Russia
Still Life with Chair Caning, 1912, Musée Picasso, Paris
Harlequin, 1918, Private Collection
Three Musicians, 1921, Philadelphia Museum of Art, Philadelphia, PA, USA

Websites

Albright-Knox Art Gallery, Buffalo, New York
www.albrightknox.org

Art Gallery of New South Wales, Sydney
www.agnsw.com

Guggenheim Museum, New York
www.guggenheim.org

Metropolitan Museum of Art, New York
www.metmuseum.org

Musee Nation d'Art Moderne, Paris
www.paris.org/Musees/Art.Moderne/info

Museum of Modern Art, New York
www.moma.org

Further reading

All the biographies listed are written for adults, but feature many reproductions of the artist's work which will be interesting to younger readers.

General

Cubism, Philip Cooper, Phaidon, 1995

Cubism, Neil Cox, Phaidon, London, 2000

The Essential Cubism 1907–1920, Douglas Cooper and Gary Tinterow, Tate Modern, London, 1983

Modern Art, Edited by David Britt, Thames and Hudson, London, 1974

Modern Sculpture, Herbert Read, Thames and Hudson, London, 1964

Shock of the New, Robert Hughes, BBC Books, London, 1980

The Story of Modern Art, Norbert Lynton, Phaidon, London, 1980

The artists

Archipenko: Fifty Creative Years, 1908-1958, Alexander Archipenko, Tekhne, New York, 1960

Georges Braque, Karen Wilkin, Abbeville Press, 1992

Georges Braque, Russell T Clement, Greenwood Press, 1994

Braque (Great Modern Masters Series) Ed. Jose Maria Faerna, Abradale Press, 1997

Visions of Paris: Robert Delaunay's Series, Mark Rosenthal, Matthew Drutt

Sonia Delaunay, Jacques Damase, Thames and Hudson, London, 1997

Sonia Delaunay: Art Into Fashion, Illustrated by Sonia Delaunay, George Braziller Inc, 1986

Art and Religion, Art and Science, Art and Production, Albert Gleizes, Frances Boulle Publishers, London, 1999

Juan Gris: His Life and Work, Daniel-Henri Kahnweiler, translated by Douglas Cooper, Thames and Hudson, London, 1969

Léger, Werner Schmalenbach, Thames and Hudson, London, 1991

My Life in Sculpture, Jacques Lipchitz, Viking Press New York, 1972

Jean Metzinger in Retrospect, Joann Moser, University of Washington Press, USA, 1990

I Am A Beautiful Monster: Selected Writings of Francis Picabia, Francis Picabia, Exact Change Publishers, 2001

Picasso, Timothy Hilton: Thames and Hudson, London 1996

Picasso, Roland Penrose: Phaidon Press, London 1991

Picasso - Portrait of Picasso as a Young Man, Norman Mailer, Little Brown and Company, London, 1996

Index

Titles in the *Artists in Profile* series include:

Hardback   0 431 11650 4

Hardback   0 431 11653 9

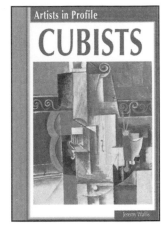

Hardback   0 431 11642 3

Hardback   0 431 11643 1

Hardback   0 431 11640 7

Hardback   0 431 11651 2

Hardback   0 431 11641 5

Hardback   0 431 11652 0

Find out about the other titles in this series on our website www.heinemann.co.uk/library